D1454036

Praise for
My Dirty Little Secrets

"Tony Mandarich's book *My Dirty Little Secrets: Steroids, Alcohol and God* is heartbreaking and heartwarming at the same time. Brutally honest at times, and always straightforward, [this is] first and foremost a great book about the power we all hold within ourselves and everything we can achieve if we only decide to do the right thing. Unfailingly optimistic, but never preachy, this book should find a wide audience of those who are curious enough to reserve judgment until they learn all of the facts. I am not qualified to say how good of a football player Tony Mandarich ever was, but he is certainly a brave man and one who can walk with his head held high anywhere in this world."

—Olivera Jackson-Baumgartner, *Reader Views*

"With the benefit of sober hindsight, Tony Mandarich has his pick of moments from a drug-fueled life that had him careening on a road to ruin. It is a chilling recollection, the chapters of both the book and his life in which Mandarich was destined for self-destruction. At least the story ends in redemption, both professionally—when he played clean and competently with the Indianapolis Colts after three years of exile—and personally, with a life dedicated to sobriety."

—Rob Longley, *Toronto Sun*

"*My Dirty Little Secrets: Steroids, Alcohol, and God* is a testament that faith in a higher power can bring us to salvation and light. Tony's story is touched by magic and brushes against the tragic. It's a great human journey and a victory for the human spirit."

—Jim Irsay, Owner, Indianapolis Colts,
Super Bowl® XLI Champions

my DIRTY *little* SECRETS
Steroids, Alcohol & God

the
Tony Mandarich Story

by Tony Mandarich, as told to Sharon Shaw Elrod

Book #5 in the Reflections of America Series

My Dirty Little Secrets - Steroids, Alcohol & God: The Tony Mandarich Story.
Copyright © 2009 by Tony Mandarich. All Rights Reserved.
Book #5 in the Reflections of America Series

Library of Congress Cataloging-in-Publication Data

Mandarich, Tony.
 My dirty little secrets-- steroids, alcohol & god : the Tony Mandarich story /
Tony Mandarich as told to Sharon Shaw Elrod.
 p. cm. -- (Reflections of America series ; 5)
 Includes bibliographical references.
 ISBN-13: 978-1-932690-77-4 (hardcover : alk. paper)
 ISBN-13: 978-1-932690-78-1 (pbk. : alk. paper)
 ISBN-10: 1-932690-77-8 (hardcover : alk. paper)
 ISBN-10: 1-932690-78-6 (pbk. : alk. paper)
 1. Mandarich, Tony. 2. Football players--United States--Biography. 3. Football
players--Drug use--United States. 4. Football players--Alcohol use--United
States. 5. Doping in sports. I. Elrod, Sharon Shaw. II. Title.
 GV939.M2875A3 2009
 616.860092--dc22
 [B]
 2008038253

Modern History Press
5145 Pontiac Trail
Ann Arbor, MI 48105

www.ModernHistoryPress.com
Modern History Press is an imprint of Loving Healing Press

Cover design and photograph by Charlavan Mandarich.
Article in *The Detroit Free Press*, April 4, 1996, by Jo-Ann Barnas, "Tony
Mandarich eyeing NFL comeback". © 1996 McClatchy-Tribune Information
Services. All Rights Reserved. Reprinted with Permission.
Sports Illustrated Cover Photo, Getty Images, April 24, 1989, reprinted
with permission.

The Reflections of America Series

The Stories of Devil-Girl by Anya Achtenberg

How to Write a Suicide Note: serial essays that saved a woman's life by Sherry Quan Lee

Chinese Blackbird by Sherry Quan Lee

Saffron Dreams by Shaila Abdullah

My Dirty Little Secrets by Tony Mandarich

"The *Reflections of America* Series highlights autobiography, fiction, and poetry which express the quest to discover one's context within modern society."

MODERN HISTORY PRESS

"Literature that is not the breath of contemporary society, that dares not transmit the pains and fears of that society, that does not warn in time against threatening moral and social dangers—such literature does not deserve the name of literature; it is only a façade. Such literature loses the confidence of its own people, and its published works are used as wastepaper instead of being read."
—Aleksandr Solzhenitsyn (1918-2008)

This book is dedicated to my Big Brother, John,

&

to the still suffering alcoholics and drug addicts. There is Hope. All you have to do is get to the jumping off place and give it a chance. After all, what do you have to lose… besides your misery?

Contents

Acknowledgements

First and foremost, I need to thank Sharon Shaw Elrod. Without you, my story would never have made it to print. Your persistence, determination, and belief that this story needed to be told started the fire and stoked the embers until the book was complete.

To my parents, Vic and Danica Mandarich; your steadfast determination, resiliency, and belief that you could create something 'better for your family' is the rock upon which I have built my life. I haven't been the perfect son, but the unconditional love you have for me is an example to which I aspire.

To my daughters; Holly, who was there during my hell, and Brittney, who wasn't. You two put the sparkle in my eye & the beat in my heart! Thank you also to their mother, Amber, for living through the rough parts with me.

To my wife, Charlavan; thank you for your help in writing, editing, and creating this book. You are one of the 'do-overs' that God has granted me, and I am grateful for your loving presence & your fearless nature in my life. A special thanks as well to my in-laws, Morris and Kay Watts for welcoming me back into their family with open arms.

To my literary agent, Irene Watson; at first I was amazed that you sold this book in 3 days, but after spending more time working with you, I can see why. Your enthusiasm, determination, and belief in what you do is an inspiration. A huge thank-you, as well, to my publisher, Modern History Press for taking a chance on me. That's all I needed: a chance.

Thank you to the Green Bay Packers & the coaches for whom I've played and the teammates with whom I've played, especially George Perles, Nick Saban, Bill Tobin, Lindy Infante, and Tom Zupancic. I'm grateful for the lessons taught and the opportunities given. A very special, personal thanks to the Indianapolis Colts organization and owner Jim Irsay, for giving me a chance.

Sometimes, all we need is someone to believe in us; I'm grateful you believed in me.

To Jim Farm & John Whyte; words are not enough to express my thanks for your friendship; you were there when I needed you most. "It ain't easy havin' pals!"

To my BEST FRIEND Kerri Dixon, you have ALWAYS been there for me!

To David Calvin, a great friend that has lived a life journey full of adversity and has chosen to take the high road of life. You'll never know how much of an example you are to me!

Finally, a special thanks to those individuals who provided guidance, assistance, and counsel in creating this book; Bill Chastain, Jerry Elrod, Ann Becker, Matthew Diddy, Mike Bowen, and Olivera Baumgartner-Jackson.

You have all become part of my story! I look forward to the next chapters...

Tony Mandarich

Foreword

The rock legend Warren Zevon once said he lived a blessed life. The first part of his life was a drug-crazed, rock star existence living on the edge. The second part of his life was one of peace and contentment, a family man who found his serenity. Tony Mandarich's journey in life would be one that would resemble Warren Zevon's path. Tony was born big, 13 pounds and 13 ounces, setting a record at the local hospital where he was born. He came into the world large. He would grow big and strong, only to dream to grow even bigger and stronger.

When he saw Mark Bavaro's biceps bulging as an early collegian, Tony would watch from the sidelines and say, "I want to be even bigger and stronger." He would become bigger and stronger: a legend at Michigan State, a pancake artist, a destroyer at the point of attack. He didn't want to just block opponents, he wanted to destroy them. He wanted to embarrass them. He wanted to take away their will. He would become one of the most dominant collegiate offensive linemen ever to play the game.

I can still remember when I was general manager of the Indianapolis Colts in 1989. As the draft neared, Troy Aikman was at the top of the board with Deion Sanders and Tony Mandarich. However, the talk of Mandarich, his dominance at such a difficult "skill position" as left tackle seemed to carry the day in some people's minds. Tex Schramm told Jerry Jones before he turned over the reins to the Dallas Cowboys, "Take the quarterback. Take Aikman." The Cowboys did, even though most teams had Mandarich graded the highest on the board. The Green Bay Packers would select him at the number two pick in the whole draft. No one was surprised. Some wondered if he should have gone as number one!

There was a ghost in the machine. Young men often show a lot of bravado in their youth. Tony would listen to Guns N' Roses and pump iron, unimaginable amounts of iron, record-setting type of lifting. He would even go out to California where the great lifters roamed. He wanted to compete against the strongest men in the world. What would it be like to train next to them? He had the feet. He had the speed. He had the strength. He had the tenacity. Sometimes offensive linemen lack that ferociousness but Tony could have played defense the way he attacked the line of scrimmage.

This ghost that lurked in the machinery would grow. If ghosts aren't dealt with, they always get stronger as we get older. That's just the nature of things. Eventually, these demons can become overpowering. They can take down even the strongest men. It takes a lot to break the will of a man, particularly a strong and proud man. Tony would enter the National Football League with high, high expectations. Greatness was expected and expected soon. He signed a huge, multi-million dollar contract that put his salary, on a per-year average, ahead of even the great, all-pro offense linemen, already veterans in the National Football League.

The pressure was too great; the demons grew and became stronger. And trouble lurked down the road for the big rookie. Rookies with high expectations and big salaries have it tough in the National Football League. The veterans wait for them. Mike Singletary once talked about preparing to go into the National Football League as a rookie. He was training with his trainer, showing fatigue, showing the lack of complete and utter desire to push it to the limit when the trainer stopped, looked at him and said, "Mike, there's a guy in Chicago who wears number 34. His name is Walter Payton. He will rip your heart out! Do you understand the level of preparedness you must endure to take on this challenge?" That's the type of difficulty rookies have coming into the league. Great players in their prime are waiting, tough veterans. The expectations are big and that makes the fall even bigger.

It's interesting in life, though, sometimes we're always focused on the answers. What are the right answers? How can we get them in our grasp? But the interesting thing is, the answers do not matter if you don't have the right questions. It's the right questions a wise man always searches for. Tony would struggle and things would not work out for him with the Green Bay Packers. Like Bob Dylan once said, "And when finally the bottom fell out, I became withdrawn. The only thing I could do was to keep on keeping on, like a bird that flew." Well, the bottom did fall out. And a difficult valley of suffering would lie ahead. The term "incomprehensible demoralization" is a very powerful phrase. Unfortunately, the words don't truly convey that dark valley of suffering that some of us must go through. Tony would exit the National Football League and, as he contemplated his future, he would watch his brother die of cancer. These were very difficult times for Tony Mandarich.

However, the real game is always the game of life. The real defining moments are played on a spiritual field. The spiritual field has many opposites that are counterintuitive to the fast lanes of life. On the spiritual field, surrender is the key. Acceptance is a virtue. Self-will has little currency on those spiritual fields of light. This is always where the great stories are written. They're written at the crossroads. The crossroads are always defined simply by God saying, "Give me your hand. Surrender your will or you will perish." This is the wonderment of Tony Mandarich's story. Some of this journey is too sacred even to be discussed. How can we find the words to describe amazing grace? Grace is not earned or fought for; grace is accepted. Grace is always available for those of us who are in the valley of great suffering. Only we can choose it. One unique aspect defines our humanity: freedom of choice. That is what we find at the diverging crossroads of darkness and light. The greatest miracles happen under the radar. The greatest miracles are the ones that are simple and humble and quiet.

There would be a complete, psychic shift, a total rearrangement within my friend who I came to know and nicknamed, "Señor." There is something so special about gentle giants; men that are so large and so strong but yet so gentle, compassionate and selfless. Tony would find his way to recovery; come back into the National Football League and play for the Indianapolis Colts and play very well. He would play against his old team, the Green Bay Packers. He would play against the great, late Reggie White and hold his own. He would compete like a National Football League starting offensive lineman who you could count on to win with. His comeback would be short-lived but still very essential. Few athletes get the chance to come back, to play well, to make things right. Tony's story is a miraculous journey of courage. It's a testament that faith in a higher power can bring us to salvation and light.

There are many aspects of Tony's story that will interest you. Most of us can only dream of being so blessed with such physical skills and dominance to play the game of football at such a high level as Tony did. Many men fall, never to rise again in this life. However, Tony Mandarich did and found a new morning. Tony remains a very close, lifelong friend of mine. A bunker mate. A fellow traveler who has helped many other people along the way. We shared our Super Bowl® victory in February, 2007 over the Chicago Bears together. We met and prayed before the game and both of us knew that we were blessed. We both realize and understand that we are not human beings having a spiritual experience, but spiritual beings having a human experience. I hope Tony's story can help others realize that we have a choice. Maybe some young man will read this book and realize what it really means to be a man. We can grow into the person we always hoped to be. We can overcome adversity and rise from the ashes. Tony's story is touched by magic and also brushes against the tragic. It's a great human journey and a victory for the human spirit.

Jim Irsay
Owner of the Indianapolis Colts
Super Bowl® XLI Champions

1	# The Rise	

An electric current ran through me when I arrived at Michigan State in the fall of 1984. Not only did I love the energy in East Lansing, I made a vow to myself: This would be my launching pad into the NFL, a dream I'd cherished since childhood. I promised myself I would do whatever was necessary to become the best football player I could be.

The game was my entire life since childhood. I'd played pickup football with my friends in my neighborhood as a child and then, at White Oaks Secondary School in Oakville, Ontario, I played organized football with equipment for the first time. Pickup football was really more my style, because we made our own rules! I was always bigger than my friends, so I was usually in charge. I loved running, competing, and most of all, I loved *winning*. The thrill of knowing I was the best in my group of friends was where the electric current in me got its start.

My parents provided another impetus for the highly charged sense of competition I developed for the game. They were role models for my belief that I had to do something extraordinary to achieve what may feel or appear like insurmountable goals. The lesson they provided me came with a high price tag for them; in 1957, they escaped Yugoslavia (now Croatia) in the dark of the night because they refused to live under Communist rule any longer. Six months after their baby girl died because they couldn't afford the medical care she needed, they left their home, taking only a small 12 by 18 inch suitcase and the clothes they wore. After walking through Croatia and Slovenia, they forged the Mura River that separated Slovenia and Austria on a cloudy night, desperately hoping the border guards with their rifles would not see them. It was their willpower and grit that finally got them to Canada as immigrants, determined to make a new life for themselves. Somewhere deep within me, I believed that if they could put their lives on the line to be free, I certainly could risk all I had to become a member of the National Football League.

Driven by my insane desire to be the best, I always sought *the edge*. My brother John, whom I revered, taught me that lesson. He said you had to have *the edge* over everyone else in order to reach your life goals. So, for me, the edge was always front and center in my plans. I sought a training regime and psychological stance that set me apart from other football players. I became unique and different because I trained differently, thought individually and prepared uncommonly. I put myself in the riskiest position possible because I fully intended to play in the NFL. Really good athletes, in any sport, are unique and different. I wanted to be the best. I wanted to become *extraordinary*.

Young and impressionable, I received a wake-up call during my first college game against Notre Dame in East Lansing. John and I had watched the Irish as kids, so I couldn't help feeling a sense of exhilaration as I thought: "Oh My God, this is THE Notre Dame! THE Notre Dame with Touchdown Jesus!" Now, I proudly wore Michigan State colors and would play against them.

Mark Bavaro added intimidation to my thoughts. Huge arms hung from the shoulders of the Notre Dame tight end; he resembled a gladiator. I weighed in at a measly 270 pounds, a stick of an offensive tackle. The mere sight of Bavaro delivered a wake-up call, the first of many that were going to happen over the next few years. I knew I had to get in the weight room to hang with the big boys. Big Time college football demanded I get serious.

Football became my twelve-month, round-the-clock pursuit. Friends went south for spring break, but I remained in East Lansing to work in the weight room. I believed championships and great players were made in the off-season. I was going to be the best player in football, whatever it took. So I spent January through April in continuous workouts and additional training programs to get the edge I craved.

Buck Nystrom, MSU's offensive line coach, ran the off-season conditioning program that began every morning at 6 a.m., which meant a 5 a.m. wake up call for me. Nystrom had more passion for what he believed in than any coach I'd ever known. Ignoring the frigid conditions in East Lansing during the winter, I walked through the dark in the biting cold weather to Jenison Field House for the morning workouts.

I wanted to play football, so I followed the rules. At least, I followed the *obvious* rules. I didn't want to flunk out of MSU, nor did I want to get kicked out for not following rules for football players. I had no concept about addictions at that point in my life, so I had no idea that in spite of my efforts to conform, I was spiraling down into a deep, dark hole. I neither realized nor admitted to myself that becoming psychologically dependent on steroids and physically dependent on alcohol was breaking all the rules and would result in a fate worse than flunking out of college. After all, everyone went out for Thursday night beer, right? Doing steroids was permissible because it would get me into the NFL. All I had to do was keep it hidden, and that made it okay. I had all the answers.

So, on the surface I did what I thought was expected of me: I studied and trained faithfully. Late afternoons found the Spartan team back in the football building, lifting weights and working out again. Sometimes we would review training material and practice our position drills, even during the off-season. My first two years included dinner in the dorm and studying in the evenings. Tutors were hired for the team, and in the evening freshmen were required to attend study hall, where the tutors were available. Upperclassmen could use the services of tutors if they chose, but if your grade point fell below 2.0, the study hall was again required. I was bound and determined I wouldn't fall below this mark, and willing to do whatever it took. I majored in communications and relished the opportunity to explore the field of journalism. That knowledge later enhanced my work as a Canadian television sports commentator and helped me to deal better with public life and the media.

During football season the routine changed. Freshmen still had study hall and all the players still had classes, twice daily practice and workouts, but the Friday nights before Saturday home games were a time filled with the tradition of decades of football at Michigan State. That night found the entire team in the Kellogg Center, an on-campus hotel where we stayed the night. Those evenings included a team dinner, team meetings and position meetings—all final preparations for the Saturday game. The curfew always came at 11:00 p.m. We each went to our room then—working, sometimes frantically, to contain the eagerness and anticipation we felt about the upcoming game. For me, Friday nights were always a preview of what I would finally have when I arrived at the door of the NFL. The anticipation of the game for me was anticipation of the NFL, and almost as exhilarating as playing on the field.

Then came Saturday mornings. As I woke up in my room in Kellogg, excitement began to grow. I went to breakfast—always scheduled at a time directly related to kickoff—feeling the thrill of the game building. Following breakfast, we showered and dressed in suit and tie. Then, several hours before kickoff, the time-honored ritual of walking from the Kellogg Center to the football field began. The contrast between game gear and suit and tie is striking, and the dissimilarity between the two was chosen on purpose: game gear is required to play the game; a suit and tie command respect, dignity and adulation. Those feelings were lost on none of us.

When we made that walk in formal attire, we always felt special, honored and respected. We'd be filthy and smelly and grimy in a few hours, but this was our time, our spotlight, during which we felt more important than anyone could possibly imagine.

Michigan State fans are passionate about football, and they let us know that every time we made that walk. Head coach George Perles led the walking parade through a tunnel of cheering fans that were hungry to see the Spartans win. The half-mile walk wove through the beautiful trees on campus, which in the fall were heavy with their riot of yellow, red and orange leaves. Making the walk was a heady experience; I always felt a rush of pride, being part of a tradition that spanned so many years.

Slowly, almost imperceptibly, I changed. I can say that now. I did not know it at the time. In retrospect, I think it probably began when I left home to spend my senior year of high school at Roosevelt High in Kent, Ohio. John and I had been talking about how to get to the NFL for years. When we were kids, we'd hurry to get our chores done on Saturdays, so we could watch college football at noon. Then on Sundays, we were glued to the television to watch the NFL game. Our shared dream was to play football in the NFL, hopefully together. We talked about what positions we would play, how we would work together on the field and how we would be the best brother-brother team ever seen in the NFL. We would have the whole world talking about us!

We knew we had better chances if we attended college in the United States. Kent State awarded John a scholarship to attend college there, and play football. During my junior year of high school in Oakville, we also talked about how to get me into a *big time* college football program. We decided my chances would improve if I attended my senior year of high school in the United States. We just had to convince our parents, and that wasn't easy. Our parents were 'hands on' parents. They had already lost a six-month old daughter, and they were determined to do everything in their power to help and protect us. They wanted us growing up 'right' and that meant going to church, serving as altar boys, no drinking, no drugs, and being watched over carefully so their strict (but loving) parental controls would ensure our safe journey into adulthood.

John was home for Christmas and New Year's of 1982-83. During Christmas dinner, John opened the discussion proposing my move to Ohio to live with him.

"Tony's really got talent and he'll have a lot better chance for a good U.S. university if he plays high school football in the States.

Colleges and universities don't recruit here, in Canada, like they do in the States." John laid out the rationale unemotionally.

Mom cried, "I can't let my boy go away. He's too young!" Dad agreed, but he also saw John's point. However, he wasn't going to argue with Mom, the matriarch of the family, at least not at first.

"But, Mom, the only thing I want to do with my life is play football," I protested, desperately needing her to give permission and equally desperately wanting to move to Ohio with John. I didn't want to leave Mom and Dad, but I *really* wanted to play football and get a jump-start to the pros. I wanted a life of my own. I wanted to fulfill my dream of being in the NFL. My parents wanted me to be what I wanted to be, but they were reluctant to let me go at the tender age of 16. They had already lost a daughter, and their oldest son had moved away. I was the only one left at home.

That discussion went on for several months. The final persuasive argument was their realization of what offered me the best opportunity; Dad finally convinced Mom to let me go, however reluctantly. She finally gave up trying to hold out against the three men in her family. My parents agreed my chances would improve immeasurably if I went to the United States for my senior year of high school.

John, only four years older than I, had to go to court in Kent to be appointed my legal guardian. And in August 1983, he and I drove from Oakville to Kent, Ohio, beginning our journey toward the goal of my NFL career. John told me we needed to seize the opportunity before it was too late. He guided and protected me and was as heavily invested in my becoming a NFL player as I was. I knew I was going to be the best NFL player ever. I would make sure everyone on the planet knew who Tony Mandarich was.

John Nemec, the head coach at Kent Roosevelt High School, and his family welcomed me with open arms. They and the other coaches and their families became my instant extended family. Here I was, a Canadian, taking the place another kid from the United States would have had on that team, yet I was accepted just like the rest of the team members. I'm still amazed that they were so giving and gracious to me. It helped make up for being away from Mom and Dad; I didn't get lonely like I otherwise might have. Even if I did, it's something I wouldn't admit. I've always felt the Nemecs didn't have to be so nice, but they were anyway, and I'll never forget that.

Again I put myself in a position most people don't normally choose. I left home and moved to Ohio with John; that was not a common thing in my culture or community. Families moved together because Mom or Dad got transferred; sixteen year-olds did not leave home for the sole purpose of getting a scholarship, improving exposure and aggressively seeking the opportunity to play big time college football. I could have gotten an education at home, but I craved more. That craving was so deep I could taste it.

My parents made a very tough decision, not only in allowing me to go live with John, but by permitting me to leave home and go live in another country, just like they'd done, but for very different reasons. It was tough saying goodbye to them, but I was so excited about the new path I was on. I had a gamut of mixed emotions. Part of me was glad to be gone because of all the strict rules my parents imposed on me—I hated rules. They often prevented expression of my rebellious nature. John had rules too, but he wasn't as strict. I was excited about the many opportunities ahead of me, but my primary thought was to play in the NFL, and I was on my way there. I didn't give any thought to the stability offered to most teens through parental control channels, but what teen does? I was singularly excited about being out from under those controls; I felt those rules impeded my creativity and movement into adulthood.

John made sacrifices for me, too. He was a college senior at Kent State, with an active social life, and suddenly he had a high school senior living with him in his apartment. That was a big sacrifice; he'd been on his own and finally away from parental rule for three years, and now... there was me. The silent question was all around him, "Your little brother lives with you?" John wanted me there for *my* benefit. That's the kind of guy he was; he was living out his role as the older brother, taking care of me. At that time I didn't fully realize the sacrifices he was making. As I think back, it touches my heart when I realize how adamantly he wanted to help me get a football scholarship and get on the road to the NFL.

On the first drive from Canada to Kent, John casually revealed to me that he used steroids, and thought it was the *edge* to get to the NFL. He said everybody in the NFL was using them. His comments were casual; I could use them if I wanted to, and if I didn't, that would be okay too. He didn't coax, didn't encourage; he just told me what he'd chosen to do to try to attain the athletic edge he thought was so important – strength beyond what you can obtain with weights.

I clearly inherited my size from my parents, but John was my older brother, and I listened to everything he told me. He was my hero and I would do everything he suggested. If he thought I should consider steroids to increase my already-large body, then I'd do it. There was no second-guessing. He said you had to be the best in your position on the team, or you wouldn't make the NFL. We both sought the best, so I started doing steroids my last semester in high school. I wanted to be the best football player in the NFL, and I would do whatever it took to get there.

I played the entire season of my senior year at Kent Roosevelt High School. I played well, and there was a lot of talk about my future in a college or university in the States. I knew I'd made the right decision about living there my senior year. One day after practice, Coach Nemec announced to the team that the coaches were going to be filming several games. We all felt important and proud, but also curious. He explained they would be sending clips of some of us to colleges and universities for possible recruiting efforts. I wanted to go to Ohio State at the time, and secretly hoped they would get some of the clips to review. If there'd been a way to ensure OSU got my clips, I'd have done it in a minute. But I didn't have any way to be sure they got them, so I resorted to praying.

Toward the end of the season, I got a call from Nick Saban, who was the Ohio-area recruiter for Michigan State University. He'd seen a game film my coaches had sent out, and he said he wanted to see me play. I was almost giddy, but I held back because a guy like me would never admit to the inner excitement—guys just didn't express feelings like that. I felt honored someone would travel from East Lansing just to watch me play football. My dreams were starting to become reality. Maybe I'd even get to visit the MSU campus. I began doing some computing… It was only a five-hour drive from there to my home in Ontario, and if I went there I would be able to see my parents more often. Maybe East Lansing would be a better place to go to college than Ohio? I could hardly contain my excitement. When he arrived, Nick told me all about MSU and said they wanted me to come to MSU for a visit. When I went to visit, they said they were interested in me playing there and offered me a scholarship. I was ecstatic! A full scholarship and only five hours from home! I could live with this deal! It was exactly what I dreamed of; I was on my way to becoming the best football player in the NCAA, and I was willing to do whatever it took.

Like all young players, I needed mentoring, and Nick knew that. He began working with me on his first visit to Kent Roosevelt High School. He was a defensive back coach at that time, and he began providing me with the counsel and direction I needed for succeeding in both college and on the university football field. There's an unspoken expectation of recruiting coaches in college football; they take players they recruit under their wings and look out for them during their college career. I was grateful for his willingness to be there for me. I actually did miss my parents, even if they did have rules I didn't like. The coaches make sure their recruits go to classes, stay out of trouble and do what's in their best interests and ultimately, the interests of the football program. I will always be the rebellious second child and I needed the help Nick had to offer. He knew me well; he knew if he didn't place an invisible guard over me, I would play out my archetypical role of being the rebel and he would have trouble on his hands.

I liked Nick. On my recruiting visit to MSU I met, and immediately liked, George Perles, who was the head coach at the time. I was told that the team was in a rebuilding process. MSU hadn't won the Big 10 Championship since 1966, and that was their goal. That appealed to my strong need to win. I wanted to be part of the winning team—I wanted to be able to brag I won the Big 10 Championship. They knew they needed to make lots of changes, and they talked with me about the ones that I'd be interested in. They told me that of the offensive linemen on the current team, I'd be close to the top in the position. I knew enough about other college teams, so that really impressed me and got my attention. I'd be down much farther on the ladder in my position (offensive lineman) at most other Big 10 schools. Few freshmen play in the starting lineup, but my chances to be a starter my sophomore year were better at MSU than at the other colleges I visited. Those other colleges already had well-established linemen and it would be tougher to break into their entrenched systems, and I *really* wanted to play. Besides, East Lansing was only a five-hour drive home. I'd been away from home since August, and I always miss Mom and Dad when I'm away from them. I didn't think I would, but I really did.

I looked at and was courted by several other colleges… University of Michigan, UCLA, University of Maryland, and a number of mid-America schools (Kent State, Akron, Ohio University, Central Michigan, East Michigan, Western Michigan, Bowling Green). Once I visited East Lansing, though, I fell in love with the town and MSU. I was impressed with what George and Nick said about where they were going. They were a "blue collar" team, not pretentious, and they were definitely well aware of the fact that they had to work to get where they wanted to be. I appreciated that; that's how I grew up. I came from a working class immigrant family, where values were placed on hard work and climbing up the ladder. Nobody in my family started at the top. I'd also been invited to visit the University of Michigan, but the recruiter was arrogant. He bragged about the U of M team and came off too superior and too proud. He told me the University of Michigan had a flag on the moon. I didn't care about flags on the moon; I just wanted to play football and get a good education.

In February 1984, after the football season was over, I spent a lot of time training in the gym in Kent. I trained 12 months a year.

At one point, I was working on the bench press and couldn't get beyond 315 pounds. Part of it was a mental block, which was related to the number of plates on the bar; three big plates on each end just *looked* like too much to lift. I complained to John about not being able to lift 315 pounds, and he said steroids would probably help. I reminded myself my main goal in life was to get to the NFL, so I told him I wanted the pills. He gave me what would be considered a very mild and small cycle of a steroid called *Dianabol*, a small blue pill (which should not be confused with Viagra). I did an eight-week cycle. Within the first month, I surpassed 315 pounds on the bench press. My strength increased significantly, probably due both to the Dianabol and because psychologically, I *believed* I was stronger. I believe I reached the next level of athletic competency faster. In retrospect, I honestly don't know which was stronger, the steroid or my belief that I was stronger.

A miserable and life-changing episode stands out in my mind from that period of time. It was a Friday night in February. We were training at the gym in Kent, and my brother and his then-lifting partner, known as ET because he was so out of this world, were working out. I was exhausted from the week of school and even though I was at the gym, I wasn't working out.

John asked, "Why aren't you working out?"

I replied, "I'm tired and just want a ride home after you and ET are done."

John and ET flew into a rage and lashed out at me, "You are an undisciplined and lazy motherf***er. If you think you're gonna be successful playing big time college football, then you're gonna get your ass kicked at Michigan State!"

After their workout, they didn't allow me to ride home with them. I had to walk three miles through a blizzard, across town and campus, to get to our apartment. This gave me a lot of time to think about my life, my goals, and what I wanted to be. Looking back, I think that was an eye opener for me, something that began preparing me for big time college football. I began to realize I had to really get serious about building strength and endurance. I needed to do whatever it took, and ignore fatigue—if I wanted to be the *best*. John was still my older brother, my hero; but he stopped taking care of me then, and I was really on my own. I had to make my own decisions and plan how I was going to be the best football player in the NFL.

Spiraling Down

Thursday night was party night at MSU, and it became my party night every week. That's when the booze was flowing. I like booze, I like the taste, and I liked drinking. A lot of in-state students attended college in East Lansing. They scheduled their classes Mondays through Thursdays, so they could have a long 3-day weekend at home. Classes were over for the week for many of the rest of us too, and it was time to have fun. By Wednesday, I was really looking forward to Thursday night.

My addictions to steroids and alcohol were slowly taking over my life. Addictions are insidious. They can be both physiological and psychological, and many addictions have components of both. I was slowly becoming absolutely dependent on steroids and alcohol for daily life and living. Psychologically I believed I needed steroids in order for my already oversized body to get even larger and stronger; it was a compulsion for me. Paranoia set in when my endurance stalled. I now know it is normal for endurance to plateau. But at MSU, in those years when my body just plain got tired, I pushed myself to do more, rather than give it a rest. In spite of the horrendous workouts I put myself through daily, I still felt it wasn't enough. I believed to the depths of my being I *had* to have steroids to become stronger, and I was so crazy-intent on getting to the NFL I didn't allow that belief to be challenged. Addictions are like that; reality gets clouded and it takes a huge *whap!* upside the head to refocus attention on reality.

However, at the same time, I was becoming addicted to alcohol.

People in East Lansing really take care of their football players. We were celebrities all over town and especially in bars, where we enjoyed privileges denied to other students. I never had to wait in line anywhere. Much of the time, food and drinks were complimentary. We were treated well, and that treatment fed my arrogance and my cocky behavior. The townspeople were showing appreciation and gratitude, and that made me feel even more special and only added to my insufferable behavior. I'd go into a bar on Thursday nights and drink free beer until I was so drunk I couldn't walk. Because of my body size I was able to consume more than a lot of my friends. Many nights I had no idea how I got back to my room, and I didn't care. I was having fun, and I was being acknowledged as a football player.

The other big party night was Saturday, especially after football games. By the end of the semester, I was in the bar every Thursday, Friday, and Saturday night. My priority had become partying. It feels strange now that at the time I did not realize I was an alcoholic. It could be because I did not know what an alcoholic was; it could be because we never talked about it at home. Yes, I do remember some people in my town that drank a lot; but they were just accepted, and sometimes called drunks. I wasn't one of *them*. But alcoholism is like that. It clouds the vision so completely that reality becomes fantasy and imaginings become reality.

That went on until January of my first year. Then I realized my performance in the weight room was suffering, and—when I had one amazingly clear-headed moment—I thought it was all due to the partying and drinking. I wasn't concerned about the effects of drinking on my body; I just worried about my performance decline and how that would affect getting into the NFL. I always thought about the NFL and how I was going to be the star player, but never about my health. As far as I was concerned, my whole career depended on my weight and size, and my strength.

I stood in front of a mirror and asked myself, "Why am I at MSU? What's my purpose?" And then I answered my own questions.

"I'm here for two reasons: get into the NFL and get an education." I got a piece of paper and wrote those two goals on it. First and foremost was to get into the NFL. Looking back now, I realize that was as much an obsession as a goal. By this time, I'd been at MSU over four months, and my determination to finish college and join the NFL was beginning to suffer damage. I needed to do some damage control, so I made a decision to slow down the drinking and partying. It still never crossed my mind that I was an alcoholic, but I made a conscious decision to slow down alcohol intake, which I did. For the rest of my college career, although I went out with friends frequently, I only drank once a month. It was just too hard to get up the next morning and workout if I'd been drinking the night before. I never smoked pot much, only three or four times a year in the five years I was at MSU. I never craved it; I just smoked it once in a while if someone in my group had it.

However, my steroid use increased during college, because I believed it aided strength and bodybuilding. I still wanted to be one of best offensive linemen in college football and I thought steroids were the way to get there. I didn't worry about the effects of steroids on my body either; I didn't care because I had one major goal in mind – to be the best star the NFL ever had.

After that list-making exercise, and through 1989 (my senior year of college), I concentrated on being the best athlete possible. I hung out with a motley crew of characters. We were all into bodybuilding and weightlifting, including taking steroids in our attempts to develop big body structures. We exuded a "bull in a china shop" attitude. I gave them information about steroids that I'd gotten from John and from my trainer in California. Some of the guys were scared of needles, so I would inject them if they couldn't do it themselves. As a result, they nicknamed me *The Doctor*. In total, my steroid use lasted six years—from the last half of my senior year of high school until my last year at MSU.

By the end of my college football career, many sportswriters said I was the best offensive lineman *ever in college football history.*[1] I was in my glory. I was on my way to the top; important people in the industry knew Tony Mandarich.

---

[1] Buchsbaum, Joel, "Scout's Notebook," Pro Football Weekly, July 28, 1996.

• • •

I didn't have much dating experience because I was always in the gym training. In fact, I've only had two serious relationships in my life—Char and Amber. One day in my sophomore year after practice, Nick Saban, my MSU mentor and one of the coaches, told me he had someone he wanted me to meet. Nick and his wife, Terry, said they wanted to introduce me to their babysitter, who had just transferred from LSU to MSU. Her dad, who also had moved from LSU, was the new offensive coordinator. Nick said he wanted to help their babysitter get acquainted and have friends at Michigan State.

Soon after, we were leaving the field after practice and I noticed a tall, beautiful girl standing by the entrance to the fieldhouse. Nick caught me and said, "Tony, this is Char Watts, the student I told you about." I'm always attracted to the beauty in women, and her beauty was stunning. She and I visited briefly, exchanged telephone numbers and I told her I would call and we'd go out. She was outgoing and bright, and I was taken with her quickly. The relationship blossomed and we dated steadily for a year and a half. She was the first long-term serious relationship I ever had.

During that year and a half, we created memories that have lasted a lifetime—me, in my 320 pound body, trying to get into Char's 300 ZX turbo, eating breakfast every Sunday after a game, and her trying to get me to see what I was doing to my body with steroid abuse. Although I was enamored with Char, I was even more enamored with myself, and how my steroid use was going to help get me into the NFL.

We played Notre Dame at South Bend in the second or third game of my third season. We were the underdogs; all the sportswriters and coaches were saying Notre Dame would win by a huge margin, and ESPN televised the game. Tim Brown, the ND wide receiver, had a heyday. He had a punt return and a kickoff return that he ran back for touchdowns. We were totally crushed. Tim was awarded the Heisman Trophy that year, and I believe that spectacular win cinched the Trophy for him. Char drove down and back in her Z with some girlfriends. She came to console me after the game. I saw her push her way through the crowd around the bus, with a determined look on her face that said, "I'm coming through here; get out of my way!" She was able to get through to the bus because her dad was one of the coaches, but that look said she'd get through even if he were not!

"Don't forget to go to Meijer for chicken wings," I reminded her. Another tradition of ours was to eat chicken wings after returning from away games. It was after 3:00 a.m. when the bus got back to East Lansing, and I really didn't expect to see her at my place. I was exhausted and it was just too late for her to be there. But both she and the chicken wings greeted my very late arrival. We fried them and talked into the wee hours. She always listened to my review of the game, and added her own thoughts. She grew up in a football family and knew a lot about the game. Even in the face of a loss, she was always encouraging—not flattering, just offering positive and realistic feedback.

I carried a sense of invincibility with me during those college years. I had no concern, and certainly no fear, about what the drugs were doing to my body and my brain. My friend Steve Ljubicic and I lived together in a trailer near campus. Char and I were there one evening. I interrupted our conversation to announce I had to take my steroids. She asked if I thought about their effects on my health. My cavalier reply was, "I'm gonna live hard and die young." I really didn't think about dying, though; I was too focused on living hard. Char was concerned about me, and I casually dismissed her query with my bravado and arrogance.

That arrogance and invincibility extended to some in-your-face behavior, not atypical for football players; mine was just exaggerated. The manufacturer's name is always stamped on the front of our helmets, above the cage of the mask. Bike and Riddell are probably the two best-known manufacturers of football helmets. Soon after I began playing in the starting lineup, I took a label maker and made a black label of my own… EVIL. I carefully placed it over the manufacturer's name. Every defensive lineman would see it when we took our stance. I wanted the psychological edge of communicating that to my opponents. Now, I'm certain steroids played a psychological effect in making that executive decision!

Many abusers report steroids significantly increase their anger and aggression. Although research on psychological effects of anabolic steroid abuse is inconclusive, abusers experience that increase when they are on the drugs. It is possible that either the effects are under-reported or there just hasn't been enough research attention given to the problem. Some researchers suggest the increased aggression and irritability are secondary to proven hormonal changes in the abuser. Whether hormonal or a direct result of taking anabolic steroids, I'm pretty sure that my abuse of steroids made me more aggressive and irritable. Alcohol abuse also contributed to that, so I had a double whammy going for me: both steroids and booze increased my level of aggression, and I had the perfect place to express it in a socially acceptable manner—the football field.

During the summer following my second year at MSU, I was preparing for football training camp. It was the July 4th weekend; I'd partied hard the previous night and had no sleep at all. The next day was searing hot. Mid-day, I began to experience heart palpitations and chest pain. My chest was tightening and the pain increasing; I was scared out of my wits. I hopped in my truck and drove to the emergency room at a local hospital. The ER docs conducted several diagnostic tests and determined my heart was okay. There were no major problems. They concluded my symptoms were a result of high stress and heat. I have since learned that steroid abuse can result in enlargement of the left ventricle of the heart. It also affects "good" and "bad" cholesterol, increasing the bad and decreasing the good, resulting in atherosclerosis, that fatty stuff that gets deposited in arteries and blocks them. I had no idea what I was doing to my body, and even if someone had told me, I wouldn't have cared. Like I told Char, I planned to live hard and die young. Nevertheless, that hospital trip was a really scary event. But it didn't stop me from continuing to drink and do steroids; I just didn't make the connection.

Winning the Big 10 Championship in 1987 was the highlight of my college career, and certainly a highlight of my life. That November we played Indiana at home. If we beat the Hoosiers that day, we'd clinch the Big 10 Championship, even though we had one game left.

We won that day, 27-3. When the clock ran out, it was absolutely stunning to see 70,000 fans rush the field and tear down the goal posts! Our win meant we'd go to the Rose Bowl, the first time for MSU since the year I was born. I was a junior, and had been named All-American; I'd also been voted the best offensive lineman in the Big 10 that year. I was on my way!

After that win, the locker room was full of roses. It was a nationally televised game, and I still have it on tape. My dreams were coming true and I was climbing to the top of my world, and now I was beginning to get national attention. The hype had begun. All my planning and hard work was paying off and I was getting closer to my goal!

Going to the Rose Bowl was phenomenal. At that time, it was the Granddaddy of them all, *the* key bowl game in the 1980s. So we knew we were the Big Game on January 1. It was Big Ten vs. PAC Ten. We played and beat USC in the Rose Bowl, proving we could do it. I was All-American and playing well, making a name for myself. I was on my way to the NFL, just a step away from being King of the Mountain. As far as I was concerned, I was going to make it.

Probably the most notorious story about my college football years occurred during a Northwestern game. My teammates and I thought Northwestern was a pitiful team. We were at the five-yard line; I drove a defensive lineman into the end zone and several yards beyond. I'd put him on his back and then looked down at him and shouted, "NOW STAY THERE!" I could feel my anger building up in me. I experienced rage with only minor provocation, and the football field is an acceptable place for expression of rage and borderline out-of-control anger.

My aggression on the field increased. We played Ohio State in East Lansing in November of my last year. The day was cold; winter approached. I was one of the captains so I walked to mid-field for the coin toss. Two of OSU's defensive linemen (tackles) were brothers, and captains that day. We met at the 50-yard line, the coin was flipped; I shook their hands, and then punched one of them in the chest, saying, "You're going to die today!" My rage was already building; I was mean and over the edge, and I enjoyed the psychological effect my anger had on my opponents. I loved the feeling of superiority I had when I lorded my strength and size over those two guys; my ability to flatten opponents like pancakes. They didn't cower; football players just don't do that. But the look in their eyes told me they weren't looking forward to having any contact with me that day. I had the ability to hurt them, and they knew it.

•   •   •

I met Amber Ligon at an East Lansing bar at the end of my fourth year at MSU. A friend knew she was going to be at the bar that night. He was interested in dating her, so he dragged me out to the bar, as if I needed encouragement to go there. The bar was one of my favorite places to hang out, even though I'd cut down on drinking since my freshman year. I knew my limits and didn't want to suffer through workouts the next day.

As planned, he got her attention and began talking, but instead of the two of them getting together, she was more interested in me. We talked a lot that night and she ended up in a relationship with me, not with him. By this time Char and I had drifted apart. Our relationship didn't really 'end' in the sense that we never told each other we didn't want to continue dating, but we developed interest in other people.

Amber and I dated for almost a year. After the Gator Bowl game in Georgia my last year, I decided to leave school early in March of 1989. I was eager to get my NFL career launched. By that time, I knew I'd be drafted; it was just a question of where I'd be in the lineup. I wanted to make one last huge effort to be ready to show the world I was the *best* football player in history. I was almost there; I literally couldn't wait to get into the NFL and I gave up my college degree to get there. Amber was eager to move to Los Angeles with me. So I dropped out of Michigan State after four and a half years, just 17 credits shy of my degree, and Amber and I headed to California.

As I reflect on some of my experiences at Michigan State, one stands out almost as if it portended the strife and grief my life would take on. After the NFL Draft every April, a supplemental draft occurs later in the spring. In 1988, I wrote a letter to the NFL Commissioner, Pete Rozelle, requesting to be included in the supplemental draft in July. I'd talked with my brother John and Vern Sharbaugh (a former coach of mine who subsequently became my agent) about going on to the NFL before my last year of college. They coaxed me to give it a try. They thought it was time for me to leave college, telling me I was good enough to play in the NFL after my junior year. They pointed out I had a chance of getting injured in college, and then not being able to play in the NFL at all. The convincing factor for me was the extra year of earning power that I would have. I was really enamored with the dollar signs in front of me, so I wrote the letter.

Then, as time went on, I became more uncomfortable with that plan, recognizing I was never as excited about it as John and Vern were. I wrote Pete Rozelle another letter, and withdrew my name from the supplemental draft list. I told him I wanted to finish college. His reply letter assured me his office had no problem with my change of mind.

However, the NCAA decided that, because I wrote the letter of request, I was a professional football player, and suspended me for the first three games of my last year of college. Those games were against Rutgers, Florida State and Notre Dame. To this day, I am unclear about how they decided I was a professional player, just because I wrote a letter. I had no agent, hadn't received any benefits and hadn't gotten paid for anything. The penalty really stuck in my craw and I fumed about it for a long time.

Steroids, Cons, and Enabling

Although drug testing began at MSU, I have a genuine hesitation exposing those experiences and the enabling environment in the football world. I don't want my words to be misconstrued or misunderstood. Then my sober mind quickly responds with, "*You cannot control the behavior of others.*" Although I cannot manage others' perceptions like I might want to, I *do* have the ability to carefully choose language to convey accurately what happened to me and who was responsible for which part of the total experience. At the age of 42 I *have* developed a conscience.

So let me say this first: My addictions are my problem and my responsibility. I was *never* forced by *anyone* to take any pill or injection or drink.

Second: I choose not to reveal names of those in my life who either participated in or enabled my addictions at the time. Although they may not have done me any favors by turning their heads and not confronting my addictive behavior, they were—and many still are—my friends... people who gave me a helping hand in other ways. They can tell their own stories. I'm not going to roll on them like that jackass Jose Canseco did.

Recovering drug addicts and alcoholics and their loved ones know a lot about co-dependent and enabling behavior. They learn about it in treatment and in follow-up support groups like Alcoholics Anonymous, Narcotics Anonymous and Al-Anon. Unfortunately, we know there are well-meaning family members and friends who turn a deaf ear to our lies, people who close their eyes to our drunken, miserable, out of control behavior. Even in the face of undeniable evidence, they make excuses for both the evidence and our actions, and behave as if our outrageous behavior is perfectly normal. In my drunken, drug-addicted world, the football industry—both collegiate and professional—enabled and hid my addiction.

Enabling and co-dependency usually go hand in hand. The co-dependent person, or in my case industry, usually has something at stake in turning a blind eye to chemically dependent behavior. A spouse, for example, may become co-dependent when s/he ignores drunken behavior in order to avoid conflict. Not confronting the behavior leads to enabling, allowing or permitting or sometimes contributing to drinking or taking drugs. Sometimes enabling behavior is passive. Ignoring behavior that you know stems from abuse of chemicals is still enabling, no matter how you want to color it.

A group of people, or an entire industry such as the NFL, has a great deal at stake with football players and their multi-million dollar contracts. It's important to have the drug testing system to show fans they are trying to police themselves. Imposing fines on violators is a strong deterrent; we hate losing money almost as much as we hate getting caught doing drugs. However, beyond the obvious efforts of the industry is a huge grey area that is cluttered with signs of drug and alcohol abuse. What should be the response of the industry when a well-known and valuable player shows signs of chemical dependency? Do coaches or fellow players have any responsibility for confronting the dependency? Or should they turn their heads and mind their own business? If my coaches and teammates were certain about my addictions, I believe that they passively enabled me by ignoring those problems.

The 1984 Cherry Bowl at the Pontiac Silverdome in Pontiac, Michigan, was my first bowl game and the only one in my college career that didn't include drug testing. I had not experienced the anxiety and dread of testing yet, so I was only aware on an intellectual level that we lucked out and didn't have to go through the ritual. It would be another year before I knew that drug testing felt like walking into a snare that could end all my dreams and hopes of joining the NFL.

The following year, the All American Bowl in Birmingham, Alabama did conduct drug testing. At that point in history, only teams going to bowl games were drug tested. The NCAA had yet to begin global and random testing.

By that year, 1985, about 15 team members and I were doing regular steroid cycles. By October, the MSU Spartans were doing so well, my teammates and I got off steroids to be able to test clean prior to the bowl game. We were taking water-based (versus oil-based) drugs and knew the approximate half-life in our systems. The steroid residue would be gone by the time we were tested in late December. Testing was done at our home school site two weeks before the bowl game. It was a simple urine test. We were given a cup, told to go into a one-person bathroom, closed the door, and came out with the sample. It was neither controlled nor monitored. But we were all clean by then, having been off the juice for two months.

The Spartan's 1987 season was great. We knew we were heading to a bowl game somewhere, and hoping for the Rose Bowl. When there were just three games left to play, I went off steroids to be able to test clean in late December. I knew I needed four to six weeks of time to get the chemicals out of my system. Since anabolic steroids don't have a euphoric effect, I wasn't aware of any psychological impact of going off the pills. I was still menacing on the field and kept my level of aggression strong; I knew how to keep the psychological edge in my favor when I played football. However, I *was* aware that I felt some strength ebbing, even in such a short period of time. I don't know if that really occurred or not. My reality-based thinking was so enmeshed with my hopes and dreams that I couldn't separate them when it came to how strong I was.

We won the Big 10 Championship and were heading to the Rose Bowl. The date for drug testing was announced; we were tested at MSU, and USC players were tested in Pasadena. I was always slightly panicked before testing, wondering if I'd given myself enough time to test clean. *Has it been long enough?* The drug stores itself in fat cells.

I'd been physically active, sweating it out. I trusted my trainer in California about timing and hoped he was right.

I tested clean and immediately went back on steroids. With certain steroids, like Anadrol-50, the user could get stronger in three days. The night after the drug test I got back on the regimen. I had two weeks to get stronger for the Rose Bowl, and I still believed I had to have the steroids to get stronger. I never trusted my ability to train rigorously, to workout faithfully and keep building my strength. It seems like I'd forever had the notion that I had to take steroids to have the strongest possible body. Again, in retrospect, I think I knew a lot of NFL players used steroids, and if they did *and I didn't,* they would have the edge and overtake me in my run for the top. I just couldn't let that happen. So I went back on a cycle that touted getting stronger in just a few days.

Two days before we flew to California, the NCAA sent a memorandum to both schools. Every player would be tested again for banned drugs in Pasadena. *Panic time!*

By that time, I'd been back on steroids for eight days and there was no way I could test clean. I was screwed. *How do I get around this?* All 15 of us considered a bunch of ways to come up with a clean test. We knew we could inject clean urine into our bladders just before the test, but most of us weren't fond of jabbing a needle into our abdomens. Blood doping was always a possibility, but very risky, especially if it didn't work right. We thought about trying to sneak a bag of urine into the testing station, but couldn't figure out how to do that and not get caught. And then a buddy of mine came up with an idea.

Another team member found the answer in a dog toy at Meijer—a squeaky toy. He made a hole in the top and another in the bottom by removing the squeakers. I practiced by filling the toy with water, taped it to my back, attached a catheter to the toy and ran it down my back and through the crack in my butt. I taped the other end to the bottom of my penis and capped the catheter with Bubblicious® chewing gum. When I removed the chewing gum and tested it, it worked. Because there was a hole in the top of the toy strapped to my back, there was no gurgling sound when I removed the chewing gum cap. *Success!*

The team flew to California on the appointed day. Upon our arrival, we were given instructions about the additional drug testing process. The NCAA had become slightly savvier by that time. No more closed bathrooms; we were required to go in a toilet stall and leave the door open. In attendance was a testing supervisor, standing behind us. There wasn't any opportunity to take a container out of our pocket and substitute it for the real thing. We had to be smarter. Drug users always have to be alert for possible dangers and interference, and have to be prepared to handle them on the spot. We carried a low-level anxiety with us constantly; the kind that knows that if we let our guard down, at any moment our dirty little secret could be exposed and we'd lose everything.

I dressed to go to the drug testing headquarters. I put on a bulky sweater so the doggie toy strapped to my back wouldn't show. I'd filled it up with clean urine donated by a teammate. My level of anxiety was ridiculous. The temperature in California in January was above 70 degrees; and yet I had this huge sweater on. I was hot; perspiration was dripping off me and running down my arms and legs, stomach and back. I really wanted a couple of beers then to just manage my anxiety, but of course that was also impossible. I was breathing fast and had to make myself slow down and take deep breaths just to get calmed down.

I entered the drug testing room and found that several of my teammates were there already. Several officials were sitting at a big table, taking information from each player. Some of the guys were dreading having to pee with someone watching, and weren't able to relax enough to be able to urinate. They were really uptight, but not from being afraid they would get caught; they just didn't want to be watched. The guys had all been standing around for 15 or 20 minutes, drinking water and apple juice, paperwork done, too anxious to be able to pee.

I walked in with my anxiety level bouncing off the ceiling. The rumors raged about my being on the juice. My denials had been printed in newspapers across the country. I was terrified of testing positive, embarrassing myself, my family, my school, and—most of all—losing my hopes for the NFL. If the squeaky toy on my back ripped off, I'd have urine running down my back. If the Bubblicious® failed, urine would run down my leg. I was trying to fill out the paperwork, sweating profusely, and suddenly felt something dripping down my back. *Oh shit. It's leaking! I have to do this NOW.*

I told the guy behind the table that I had to pee right now, making it sound urgent. He must have believed me, because he gave me a cup and signaled for a supervisor to follow me to the toilet stall. I unzipped, pulled off the Bubblicious® and the clean urine flowed into the cup. No bubbling or gurgling noises. The squeaky toy peed clean urine without a hitch. I was in the clear!

As soon as I capped the cup sample and gave it to him, I knew he didn't know. I zipped up and walked back to the table, engaging in small talk with the supervisor, which confirmed even further that he didn't know. I finished the paperwork and walked out.

The relief of stress was as ridiculous as the anxiety itself. We won the Rose Bowl game that year, beating USC 20-17.

I got cocky. My teammates and I beat the drug test with a doggie squeaker and some Bubblicious®. I had a year to practice how to beat the drug tests, so I decided to not even get off the stuff the following year; I decided early on to just cheat again. It's still unreal to me that we got away with it. Some folks in charge had to have their heads turned. I certainly can't prove they did, but the clear vision of hindsight tells me that with 15 of us using a squeaky toy to pee clean urine, there had to be some evidence left behind somewhere, and someone had to see it. Enablers generally neither recognize nor understand their supportive role in chemical dependency. The 15 of us took on the NCAA with a doggie toy and some *Bubblicious*®, and we won.

The second cheat was easier. I had a year to think about it and practice. Some guys were planning to do blood doping or inject clean urine into their bladder an hour before testing. A few guys got the protocol on blood doping and decided to risk being able to do it right. Others would use the needle on themselves, injecting clean urine; still others cringed at the sight of a needle. They got another guy to do it for them so they did not have to look. I did not relish the idea of anybody sticking a needle through my abdomen into my bladder, so I came up with another idea.

I got a large Elmer's® glue bottle; the tall one with the cap that opens and closes with half a turn. The thick elastic band of my jock strap held the bottle tight against my abdomen. I'd made a slit in the strap for the orange cap to go through and capped it closed after I'd filled it with clean urine, donated by a friend on the team who wasn't doing steroids. The urine needed to be warm because by this time, the NCAA was also testing the temperature. I kept the Elmer's® glue bottle of urine warm next to my body, so the temperature would be the same.

For the Gator Bowl in 1989, I'd practiced the cheat enough that my anxiety level was only slightly elevated. I knew it would work. In the toilet stall, supervisor behind me, I unzipped, turned the orange cap a half turn, squeezed the bottle to empty the urine in the cup, making sure to turn the cap closed before I let go of the bottle so it wouldn't emit any noise. It even sounded like I'd peed. I pretended to shake off excess urine, gave the cup to the supervisor and zipped up. The caps were tight, so I knew they wouldn't leak urine down my legs. That was the cheat for the Gator Bowl. Simple, easy, and it worked. I was hooked on cheating and I knew I had accomplished a feat. The year before I had beaten the NCAA with a doggie toy and Bubblicious®; this year it was with a high tech bottle of glue I bought at a grocery store. The NCAA punished me for writing an innocent letter when I was a junior, but all my cheating and conning was totally ignored. The irony of the contrast is inescapable. However, I was still on the road to the NFL.

The NCAA Drug Testing program today is administered by the National Center for Drug Free Sport. The 20-page manual outlines procedures for testing, re-testing if banned substances are found, appeals procedures and recommendations to institutions regarding their in-house drug testing programs. In the 20 years since my Rose Bowl escapade, a lot has been accomplished toward ensuring athletes are drug-free during competitive sports activities. Do athletes still use steroids and drugs? Of course they do. They have just gotten smarter about hiding it.

My days of steroid use ended soon after my departure from MSU. I'd signed a contract for a million dollars a year, and if I were suspended for four games because of a dirty drug test, I'd be fined and lose a lot of money. I didn't want the suspension and I didn't want to pay the fine. On a secondary level, I also didn't want to be concerned anymore about heart and liver damage, side effects of steroid use. I had begun to allow the reality of the physical side effects of steroid use into my consciousness. I knew it could lead to tumors in the liver, heart attacks and stroke. At some point, I decided I did not want to deal with all the negatives that were becoming possibilities, so I stopped using steroids. I never cheated on a drug test in the pros and I was off steroids for good.

However, lurking around the next corner was the mother of all addictions, the one that would create the ruin of my NFL dreams. My steroid abuse would pale in comparison to what was waiting for me. I had not reached my goal yet, and the cover over the black hole I leapt into slammed shut behind me. I didn't even hear it.

The Body Building Cult

I moved to Los Angeles for one reason only; I wanted to train with the *best* trainer I could find, and that's where he was. Because I was so focused on the NFL, I continued to be obsessed with being the best. The trainer prepared a schedule and diet for me. It included about 15,000 calories a day and workouts that were grueling. I'd found him 24 months prior to moving, and we communicated by telephone and mail. He was the resource I used for my final training push before the draft in 1989.

Eating was a priority, and I liked that because I always liked to eat. My mom was, and still is, the best cook I've ever known. So I ate a lot in those days; the nourishment supported all the hours of training I did every day. My calorie count was undeniably high. I really DID eat seven meals a day; I was always hungry because I was always working out.

I'd whipped my body into top-notch shape at a price. Within a few weeks, constant pain racked my body. I hurt all over, every day, as a result of the punishing workouts I constantly put myself through. I told my trainer about it and he instructed me to stop by his house after workout one day. He said he had something for my pain. When I arrived, he produced a syringe and told me he would inject me with some stuff that would make the pain go away almost instantly.

As I pulled up my shirtsleeve to expose my arm, he said, "No. In your veins."

I jerked my arm away and cried, "I'm not a damned drug addict!"

He assured me, "This is just for your pain. Trust me." And I trusted him. The pain disappeared immediately. The euphoric high was incredible, *intense*. The hook was immediate. All the drama in my life went away; problems and people and expectations that I couldn't live up to. Everything became okay in my life. Stadol was the answer. I couldn't believe the transformation.

After just a few days, the more I got, the more I wanted. He'd just introduced me to mainlining painkillers. (Mainlining refers to injecting drugs directly into the blood stream.) This type of addiction has annihilated thousands of men and women; the famous, infamous and just plain human. It disguises itself in pain-relief. In reality, it is brutal, vicious and deadly; one of the cruelest of jokes played upon humankind.

My first few months in Los Angeles, I worked out nonstop, and did my last cycle of steroids. After the draft that spring, though, I stopped performance enhancing drugs (steroids), because the NFL tested randomly for it. I simply couldn't take the risk. If I got caught, I'd be fined and miss playing games. I also didn't want a national media fiasco, which would surely have ensued if I ever tested positive. Steroids produce a definite physical effect, increasing muscle mass. They don't produce athletic skills, but they do increase strength. Basic athletic ability has to be present first. As a result, when I stopped using them, the psychological effect created more damage for me than the physical effect. I *believed* I was getting smaller and weaker. I felt like the incredible shrinking man. I became short-tempered with everyone. The irritability continued even after I stopped taking cycles of steroids; it became part of my personality, rather than coming to a halt when the drugs were no longer in my system. All my relationships were affected by my shriveling self-image.

However, the first four months of training in California, before I began injecting painkillers, I got my body into the best shape of my life—ever. I trained, worked out, ran... I was very fit. Those four months were truly euphoric for me. I knew how I looked, and how I felt. I was in great physical condition when my trainer introduced me to mainlining, still on my way to the NFL. The draft was coming up and I knew I'd be drafted high on the list.

The National Football League created the Combine to assess and rank performance and ability of individual players who are likely to be drafted. Draftees work out (perform) for NFL teams two to three months before the Draft. Because I was expected to be among the first drafted, I had my own Combine and the NFL scouts came to me. I was in great shape and performed really well; some news stories reported Herschel Walker was the only NFL prospect that had ever done better.

However in April 1989, I went from my first initial injection of painkillers to 5 or 6 a day within a single week. That continued every day for the next 3 years. The physical deterioration began almost immediately. I could see it and feel it and I thought I was helpless to do anything about it. I was immediately so hooked on the painkillers that my obsession with being the best began to deteriorate along with my body. What became the primary goal in my life was getting the drugs and shooting up. With that great hindsight vision, I now realize I was becoming the *best mainliner* I could be.

The trainer also introduced me to a growth hormone, which I took for a twelve-week period during my time in California. The combination of all the drugs was lethal to my athletic drive. I soon became lethargic and lazy. Training became immensely difficult and I lost focus in my life. Mainlining, no more steroids, hormones and chemicals, and always beer and liquor... The deadly downward spiral had begun in my life. I was on a steep downward slope in a vehicle that had no steering wheel or brakes.

My trainer and I had a falling out in the last few months of the summer I was living in Whittier, where we trained. I believe his jealousy of the national attention I received finally surfaced. I haven't spoken to him since. I don't point the finger at him for any of my usage of HGH, steroids, or painkillers. I was the one who ultimately made the decision to do all of those things. I don't blame him or hold him accountable. He was simply my introduction.

• • •

I turned into a master negotiator that summer. I'd given some serious thought to trying to go after a bodybuilding title in the future, after I achieved and finished my NFL career. In the process of some preliminary exploration of that, I came across another opportunity, a possible heavyweight championship fight with the then-heavyweight champion of the world, Mike Tyson. Some of the press ridiculed that at the time, but the talks really did happen. There actually was a serious run to set the fight up through promoter Shelley Finckel and boxing trainer Lou Duva, who also trained Evander Holyfield at the time. They flew out from the East Coast to Los Angeles to meet me and work me out, to see if I had the raw skills to fight that fight. The gym I worked out in at the time, Uptown Gym, was a dive in Whittier, CA, but had all the equipment that a serious lifter would want, albeit in a dungeon-like atmosphere.

I was already at the gym when three white stretch limos pulled up. I was introduced to Lou Duva and Shelley Finckel; from there we went to lunch and got to know each other better through small talk. We all agreed they would take a look at me to see if I had what it takes to make it a good fight. The next day, a Saturday, they set up a workout for me with Lou at a boxing gym in Englewood, the heart of gang territory, from 8 a.m. until noon. Lou worked me out for two solid hours. I didn't realize what shape you had to be in to box in the ring, and I wasn't even getting hit. I knew, though, that I was showing them I could fight Mike Tyson or anybody else who carried a champion title. I was really pumped after that workout and I knew I'd given them a good show. I was incredibly strong and wanted them to think I was the *best*, maybe even better than Tyson.

After the workout Lou said, "You have the raw skills to fight this fight, but the fight won't last more than three rounds, because either Mike will kill you, or you will kill Mike." I believed him. If I fought Mike Tyson, we'd both go for the kill. Whoever won would just be the guy who got lucky.

I remember that when we left the gym, there was a crowd of furious amateur boxers/gangbangers who were wondering who the 'm—f—' was who had closed down their gym and blocked the street with white stretch limos. They were really pissed off and we had to walk out into the middle of them to get back to the limos. Their hot and angry looks could have melted ice. It was a tense walk through that pack back to the limos; they were vicious and menacing, fists clenched at their sides, yelling profanities at us, like angry dogs growling just before they charge their prey. They were all dressed for workouts in the gym, and we had obviously interfered with their plans. I was hoping we wouldn't have to demonstrate our fighting skills on the street.

A couple of months before the draft, Rick Telander, a sports writer with Sports Illustrated, traveled to Whittier to interview me. He spent about a week following me around, and I eagerly anticipated seeing the article and pictures. I was flabbergasted when the April 24 edition showed up on newsstands all over the country, with me on the cover. It was a full-body shot taken on Venice Beach at sunset, with bulging muscles all over my body. Steroid-fueled muscles. I was speechless.

I happened to be at LAX a week later. As I walked past a newsstand, I saw 50 copies of that SI edition displayed across the top shelf of the bookstore. I was astonished to see so many images of myself displayed so prominently in such a public place. I recognized then that I was an item for the national press, *big time national press*. That was another heady experience, fueling my arrogance and sense of superiority. I really began to grasp the fact that now, finally, after all the years of dreaming and subsequent years of training and working out, I would achieve the stature I so desperately craved. I would definitely, for sure and certain, without any doubt, be drafted into the NFL. I would, finally, be crowned with the glory of playing in the National Football League.

About a week later, I appeared on the David Letterman show in New York City. I knew then that I was not only a national sports figure, but I was also a nationally recognized personality. We talked about my life—diet, football, the SI article, Tyson fight, and steroids. My standard reply was always, "I have never tested positive for drugs." That has remained my reply, until I decided to tell this story.

But I had taken steroids at MSU, and I got coy and cocky and cheated instead of revealing the truth. As any good politician does, I avoided answering the question with a statement in response to a question unasked. The guys in Washington, DC do that all the time. I could do it too.

I don't remember when I came up with that phrase. But I do remember that, once I said it, I clung to it and repeated it every time I was asked about my steroid use. Until now, I have never publicly admitted to taking steroids. Who would choose to remain on the railroad track with the oncoming locomotive barreling toward you at 120 miles an hour? We run, hide, duck, leap out of the way of total destruction instead. Admitting to taking steroids would have cost me everything at the time, so I didn't admit it. I lied to the press and I cheated on drug tests. What a miserable, stinking mess I'd fallen into. Or maybe I'd jumped in headfirst and lost all sense of the reality into which I'd sunk.

I was in New York City for some television appearances. As I walked down the street heading toward the television studio, a passerby looked at me, took a second look and then broke out into a big grin.

"You're Tony Mandarich!" Keeping my sense of exhilaration hidden inside, I smiled and saluted in acknowledgment. Strangers on the street recognized me! I loved all the attention that seemed to come from every quarter in the country. I was famous. Everyone knew me. The attention and hype meant I was one step from the top. I was within striking distance of my goal. My hand was closing around my goal, *being the best football player in the NFL and perhaps even in football history!* There was so much hype by this time that I became hooked by it. I was beginning to believe what sportswriters were saying, that Tony Mandarich was the best offensive line prospect ever. I was living in all the spectacular fantasy that was being created about me, and I contributed to that creation whenever I could.

I also did a cameo appearance on the sitcom *Dear John* that spring. I played a football player whose girlfriend was cheating on him. It was a really funny skit and I had lots of fun doing it. Although I had a short script to follow, I was allowed to ham it up and pretend I was really angry and hurt that I'd been cheated on. I remember making it look like here I was, a big bad football player; why in the world would any woman choose to cheat on me and go out with someone else? After all, I was the superior choice!

Pat Sajac had a nighttime show that season, and invited me to appear. As with the David Letterman show, we talked about football, my diet, the Sports Illustrated article and the possible Tyson fight. Those television appearances, individually and collectively, drew a lot of attention my way. I've been told that even football-impaired people knew who Tony Mandarich was. I was big, had distinctive features (genetically driven from my Croatian background), and I knew how to get attention. My bulky muscles were obvious, even when I was fully dressed. Everyone knew who I was.

Later that spring, I was still negotiating with both Green Bay and the boxing promoters at the same time; Green Bay must have felt a sense of urgency to get the deal done, and they did. The fight fell by the wayside. Disappointed? Maybe just a little. A fight between Mike Tyson and me would have been like him stepping onto the football field in pads and going up against me in a drive block. He probably would have beaten me, it was his game, but he did lose for the first time in his next professional fight with Buster Douglas; and I later realized, with mild regret, that he might have been ripe for the picking.

I held out signing the contract through all of camp. The draft was in April, but I didn't sign until September 5, 1989. I was trying to get the best contract I could from the Packers organization, but I was also losing my athletic drive because of the drugs. I began to be so focused on getting them, that my energy was no longer centered on being the best player in football history. Drug addiction is particularly dangerous because the body's need for the chemicals escalates over time. There comes a point where the body is no longer satisfied with what it's getting, and it cries out for more—sometimes with pain and sometimes just with a horrendous craving that can't be satisfied until the next fix. So I began to spend my days shooting up, and then planning for the next hour when I could repeat the injection. Doing the painkillers had replaced my intense, lifelong drive to reach the NFL, and my new addiction was just as powerful in my life as the NFL goal had been for years. Probably even more so, because I clearly believed I could not live without mainlining.

Green Bay and I finally agreed on a four-year contract for 4.4 million dollars, making me the first offensive lineman in NFL history to make a seven-figure salary. I'd finally made it, and became a millionaire in the process! The reality of finally reaching the goal John and I had created so many years ago sunk in. I was *there!* I had finally reached the pinnacle and believed my entire life was laid out before me. I could do anything I wanted now, because I had arrived. I was mainlining painkillers half a dozen times a day and couldn't see the damage this was already doing to my body. My addiction to painkillers was already clouding my vision, distorting the destruction it wreaked.

I finally signed with Green Bay on September 5th. The holdout due to contract negotiations, which caused me to miss all of camp, definitely hurt my introduction into the NFL. I hadn't practiced with my teammates at all because I was holding out for a better contract. They had been working together since April; the four to five months I missed meant I wasn't ready to play in the first game. I'm the only one responsible for that. September 5th was the Wednesday before the first Sunday game; I was neither mentally nor physically ready to play and the coaches knew it. They put me on a two-week roster exemption so I could catch up. I began to get caught up with the team those two weeks, training with them and trying to figure out how to play with an entirely new set of players. Even though we always had plays to follow, different players interact a little differently, and I had to figure all of that out. This was the first time I was on the field since becoming addicted to painkillers, and I knew my timing was off and my strength had diminished. Yet I couldn't focus; the painkillers interfered even with that.

My first game after I signed was at home, against the New Orleans Saints. I remember that our fullback, Brent Fullwood, had on shoes with only half-inch cleats. After the first two series of plays in the game, he was slipping all over the turf. He told the equipment guy he needed other shoes with ¾ inch cleats. The equipment guys were busy; they had other stuff to do first. Brent said he needed them the next time he went on to the field, so I said that I'd go get them, if he would tell me where they were. He told me how to find them in the locker room.

I started walking down the sidelines into the tunnel to get Brent's shoes and the stadium erupted into cheers. They assumed I was going to get pads on and come out and play in the second half; there was that much hoopla in the media about me coming to Green Bay. The fans were screaming, thinking I was getting suited up to help the Packers win the game.

I ignored them. It was nonsense and I knew it. There was no way I could play after holding out and not training for five months. I really wanted to play, but even that drive had lessened. I'd spent a lifetime getting ready for this moment, and the desire—although weakened by drugs—was still there. All I wanted to do was play football. Although I ignored the fans, it felt good to hear them demanding I get out on the field and kick ass.

I didn't know it yet, but with my addiction to drugs, my physical and emotional stamina was seriously impaired. The strength in my muscles had deteriorated. I wouldn't be able to play well for several years.

I got Brent's shoes, took advantage of the time to shoot up again, and returned to the bench.

My reflections on that moment reveal the façade of the time. Tony Mandarich resurrecting the Green Bay offensive line was such a joke. Being the 'best offensive lineman' in history was pathetic. If I'd told them I was a drug addict back then, nobody would have believed me. The hype that had been created about my draft was total bull. There wasn't any way *anybody* could have lived up to all the expectations that were created for me and by me. It was impossible.

I played the third game of the season against the Rams in Los Angeles at Anaheim Stadium. I didn't start but I played quite a bit... not great, not horrible... just okay. I had finally achieved my goal; I was playing in the NFL, but my downfall had already begun and I was spiraling down, picking up speed on the way.

Blurry in Green Bay

A supermarket in Green Bay invited me to do an autograph session. They offered me a reasonable amount of money, and even complied with my request to throw in 10 rib-eye steaks. Green Bay was one of my last choices, because it is such a small market, and I wanted to make sure I'd get a big contract to make it worthwhile. Market size is an issue for every national sports figure, but no one talks about it publicly because we sound greedy if we do. Big markets like Los Angeles, New York City and Miami provide many more endorsements and perks. Because Green Bay is small, big endorsements aren't available; I'd miss out on financial opportunities in that market. I wasn't very excited about doing ads for cheese, bratwurst and paper mills.

I soon discovered, however, that I was a big fish in that small pond at that time. I liked that position, because it meant I was at the top of the heap, and I enjoyed being there! Several other circumstances also helped. I was on the cover of Sports Illustrated, outspoken, had national recognition, and was the second pick in the draft. All that helped me generate lots of autograph sessions and requests from companies. I profited financially and free products abounded. All I cared about was getting rich and keeping my drug supply lines open, and I didn't care how loud I had to be to get there. My biggest mistake was not caring enough about football.

Great athletes and great players can make adjustments in style of play. When I got to the NFL, I saw the speed of the game was considerably faster than college football, a significant change for a rookie. But I had more than game speed to deal with.

A comment reflected historically by Joel Buchsbaum in 1996 described my diminished physique: "When he reported to Green Bay, he was just a shell of the man and player he had been in college and seemed to lack the strength and agility needed to play in the NFL."[2] Buchsbaum noted that I was 6'5", 310 pounds and ran a 4.8 40-yard dash, and set weightlifting records right and left in pre-draft workouts. I had lost more than 30 pounds during my holdout, and my entire life kept skidding down that dark nasty hole, with no hands on the controls.

I missed all of camp and immediately faced a complex offensive system that was foreign to me. The NFL, and particularly Green Bay, is more pass-play than run-play oriented, which meant I had to learn to play in a system that passed the ball much more than ran it. All my life I've played on teams where the opposite ruled. When I finally mastered the program, my style adjusted in the process, but I was just too high most of the time to play well. The high came from drinking and drugs, not steroids. My system was so overpowered by the painkillers and booze that I couldn't keep my muscles and reflexes coordinated enough to do justice as an offensive lineman. The chemicals created interference and that meddling increased by the day. Most painkillers on the pharmaceutical market today are central nervous system depressants. That means they decrease the ability of the brain and circuit of nerves throughout the body to do their job. No matter how much I willed my body to do what I wanted, it had already lost the ability to respond.

Thus, the adjustment to the NFL was much more difficult than I thought it would be. I thought my abilities would just *do it* for me, but looking back, I was pulling on both ends of the rope. I was pulling myself down with mainlining and drinking while I was trying to pull myself up to achieve my goal of being the best at the same time. The coaches started me on a two-week exemption list because I had so much to learn, so I wasn't on the starting lineup. The exemption list meant I didn't count against their roster. In week

---

[2] Buchsbaum, Joel. "Scout's Notebook." *Pro Football Weekly.* July 28, 1996.

three, I was put on the active 53-man roster, and I was used in a limited role on short yardage, goal line, and special teams. It was frustrating, but I now know that my addiction and dependency were starting to dominate both my performance on the field and life in general. As my frustration grew, so did my irritability. I was having difficulty focusing on playing football, and because I wanted so desperately to play well, the internal conflict that resulted kept me off balance emotionally. First I wasn't playing; then, when I was playing, my performance was off; then it became just plain poor. That deflated my ego, and my sense of failure began to grow. I became easily irritated, flying off the handle and blaming everyone in the world for my trouble but me.

A lot of the coaches had a sense of urgency, because they wanted me to succeed. One coach, Charlie Davis, spent an incredible amount of time with me in his efforts to help me get caught up in training early on. I'd missed both training camp and regular summer training because of my contract holdout. Charlie seemed to make it his personal mission to review training drills, explain strategy and help me learn the new material specific to the Packers' organization. Everyone seemed to be going above and beyond the call of duty to help me.

The reaction from the team was not always so supportive. A lot of the offensive linemen resented me for making so much money and not performing. That resentment is normal and I understand it. However, the size of my contract helped them the following year in their own contract negotiations; at the time, I expected gratitude for that – but of course, didn't receive it.

Little did I know that this was the beginning of four years of shame, embarrassment and disgrace, for fans, friends, family, and myself. I was so constantly doped up by the drugs that the reality of the humiliation didn't hit until much later, when the drugs were finally wiped out of my system.

My style of play prior to the NFL was simple. It was a style that George Perles brought into Michigan State from the Pittsburgh Steelers championship teams of the 1970s. It was in-your-face, smash-mouth football, and the style suited me just fine. At Michigan State we were a run-oriented offense, probably 80 percent run and 20 percent pass, and of the pass, most of it was play-action; that style of offense suited me perfectly.

In the NFL, I went to a system where it was 60% pass and 40% run. Had I been sober, I could have accommodated the change. When I was sober, I trained well and learned quickly. But I was a drug addict and alcoholic, in complete and total denial, unable to make the necessary adjustment. I found myself in a daily struggle to keep up the front. I was numb, trying to get high constantly, so that I could live up to the expectations I believed everyone in the country held about me. I was the second pick in the draft, and that meant I had to excel *every* time I ran onto the field. I could never make any mistakes. Tony Mandarich was beyond making mistakes. What hype I had come to believe!

I tried desperately to maintain the perfect buzz during my waking hours. I was a part time professional football player, and full time drug addict and alcoholic. My addictions totally controlled my life, and as I began to experience my inability to live up to all the expectations, a vicious cycle developed. The more I drank and drugged, the worse my performance on the football field became. And the worse my performance was, the more I drank and drugged in my vain attempts to handle the disappointment and growing grief in my life.

I had several sources for prescription painkillers. Early in my Green Bay years, I met a physician at a social event. He was a big fan and appeared to be intoxicated with my celebrity status. When I learned he was a physician, my heart began beating faster. I thought, *"He could be another pipeline for prescriptions."* I knew if I handled it well, he could become a major source for the drugs my life depended on.

After we exchanged small talk, I put a sincere, questioning look on my face. "You know, I just thought of something... you are a doctor and you might be able to help me." I counted on all the stars in his eyes as he looked at me. I continued, "I have a back injury. It's chronic. I can play, but it hurts constantly. Would you be able to provide a prescription for me for Fiorinal #3?" I was as subtle as my 310-pound bulk could manage.

"Doesn't the team provide that for you?" He bought my story.

"Yeah, but they don't give me as much as I need," I said, communicating my understanding of the limitations of the team docs.

He didn't miss a beat. He was in awe of me and responded, "No problem! I'll take care of you!" The bright light of my stardom dazzled him for over two years. I took care of him, too, with tickets and autographed jerseys and helmets. He was a fine physician, a genuinely great guy, and I conned him mercilessly. There was always a lot of reading between the lines. Read my eyes; I'll take care of you if you take care of me. He wrote me a prescription for 100 pills a month for two years. Soon I began filling them early, telling the pharmacist I had to go out of town and needed an early refill. Lying and conning had become my daily habit.

In my last year at Green Bay, I pushed the doctor for another prescription soon on the heels of the last one. He put up his hand and said, "I think you might have a problem with these drugs. I can't keep giving you this stuff. Your health is suffering and I'm really concerned."

"Hey, you're my friend!" Panic began to grow in my gut. I frantically searched for another con.

"I have to be careful as a physician; all this is recorded on my DEA number." His concern for me and for himself showed all over his face.

"Then give me samples!" I was relentless. I *had* to have the pills. He caved in to my pressure and gave me both samples and another prescription for 100 Fiorinal #3 a month. And that still wasn't enough.

One day when I stopped by his office to get another script, he spoke very firmly, "Tony, you're my friend and I care about you. So I'm cutting you off. I'm not going to give you any more samples or any more prescriptions. You need help!"

Although I contained my fury, I'm sure he could see it in my eyes. All I could think about was the loss of this dependable lifeline. The painkillers my body depended upon were being cut off. *Oh my God!* Panic set in quickly.

"I thought you were my friend," I spat out. "I took care of you, gave you tickets and autographed stuff, and now you're paying me back with pain and suffering! Why would you cut me off?" I spat out the words, volume increasing with each phrase. My anger boiled just below the surface. Where in hell was I going to find a lifeline like this one had been?

"Tony, I *am* your friend, and that's why I'm not going to provide you with painkillers that are creating such a huge problem in your life. I also don't want to create problems for my career, myself and my family." He was resolute. I spun around and walked off, vowing never to speak to him again. It was a slap in the face and I couldn't understand why a friend would cut me off. I was absolutely hysterical because the lifeline was gone. I knew I had to find another one, and soon.

Assistant trainers also provided pills for me. They weren't in awe of me like the physician was, but I took care of them as well. I had a suite in the stadium with four tickets, and I gave assistant trainers tickets as long as they hooked me up with painkillers. Team docs examined players every week for injuries, and everything got recorded in a book, including medications provided to the team members. Assistants disbursed pills prescribed by team physicians. One assistant in particular would always give me more, when I asked him for it. I'm not sure how he massaged the information he recorded in the book, but he gave me all I asked for and probably wrote down that he gave them to other guys. It was another lifeline for me. And I didn't have to do much lying or conning to get what I wanted from this source.

Because of the numbness from drug use, playing football was not the priority it had been twelve months prior to that time. I was now in a position where I was mainlining six or seven times a day. And it had become the focus of my waking hours. I was either high or getting high. If I was not getting high, I was getting the stuff to get high. I wasn't living up to my expectations of my NFL career, and I didn't really care all that much. I wasn't living up to other peoples' expectations of my career, and they cared a hell of a lot more. Drug and alcohol addiction replaced my NFL career goal, and I didn't care.

I did learn the system and ended up starting for two years, but I was never 100 percent committed to my employer, the Green Bay Packers. I should have been that way the whole time, but drinking and drugging had become the priority and focus in my life. I was on a slow road to hell on earth, and there were no detours or turnarounds along the route.

I managed to convince myself the drugs helped me, and helped my performance on the field. Drugging took the pressure off, and I thought I played better. Truth was, drugging absolutely didn't help one bit. It hurt me, sent me into a vicious cycle of desperation that ended in a black void and robbed me of everything I ever wanted.

I'd been leaving the syringe and Stadol in my pants in my locker during practice when, one day, some teammates got suspicious. After practice that day, I went into the locker room and got the stuff out of my pants hanging in my locker. I went into the bathroom stall, drew the syringe and gave myself a shot. A teammate followed me in there, peeking through the crack in the door. I caught him; he was trying to see what I was doing, and he tried to cover it up.

"Can I help you?" I asked, annoyed and demanding.

"No, just checking for an empty stall." He was obviously lying. We'd never gotten along. But the whole thing was a circus. I was trying to cover my tracks, and he was trying to catch me. It was one big merry-go-round. My irritation was obvious and out of control. I'd make life difficult for him if I could. After that, I left the paraphernalia in my truck in the parking lot, and I'd go out there to shoot up during practice when I needed my next fix. I didn't see that cheating on myself like that was a thousand times worse than cheating in drug testing.

A few months later, I became so paranoid about other players finding out about my drug abuse that I stopped leaving it any place where it could be found. If anyone had become suspicious, they could check my locker when I was out on the practice field, or follow me to my truck. We practiced outside, not in the indoor facility. If a player needed to go to the bathroom, he had to run to the inside john; too many fans were watching to take a leak outside.

So I started keeping the stuff in my pants. My practice shorts didn't have any pockets, so I put a 10cc bottle of Stadol and a syringe in my jock strap. When I needed a fix, I'd take a bathroom break, go inside, shoot up and then get back on the field, loopy as hell. With the thick elastic of my jock strap holding it in place, I went through NFL practice day after day with drugs and a syringe in my crotch.

In late 1990, we played the Philadelphia Eagles at Veteran's Stadium on a national Sunday night ESPN game. It was my first encounter with the 'Minister of Defense', Reggie White. What many had touted as being a key match-up of two Titans battling for 60 minutes was almost nothing; Reggie White tossed me around like a rag doll all night. I had given up three sacks, and countless amounts of pressures to the quarterback, Don Majkowski. I hoped I would never meet up with Reggie White again, but I realized during April of the next year, when the NFL schedule was announced, that we opened up with Philly at home at Lambeau Field… and that meant another match-up with Reggie White.

That day was different. By no means did I dominate Reggie White; however, I did hold him to zero sacks, and played a decent game against him. But there is a story within this story: I had a backside cutoff block on Reggie, which is an easy block for me because of my physical strength. I was cutting him off, doing what I thought was a good job, but I didn't know the running back was going to cut back my way because the lead side had gotten stacked.

Reggie made the tackle for no gain, which lead me to stand up and yell "GODDAMMIT" at the running back. Reggie grabbed me by my shoulder pads, looked me in the eye, and said, "Son, God had nothing to do with it."

As I shrank to about 4'11", I said, "Yes sir, Mr. White", and sulked back to the huddle.

We played the Arizona Cardinals at Sun Devil stadium in 1991. After I'd dressed for the game, I went into a stall in the bathroom and slammed eight pills full of caffeine and barbiturates. I'd taken so many so often by then that I could swallow them without any liquid to wash them down. They were capsules, and they slid down my throat as if my stomach had eagerly prepared the way, anticipating the buzz my body constantly required. That was before pre-game warm-ups. At halftime, I slammed eight more and played the remainder of the game high as a kite. After the game, I mainlined when I got out of the shower, in a bathroom stall in the locker room, before the long flight home. I needed the painkilling drugs to calm my system down (after the caffeine and barbiturates) and get me mellow and relaxed for the long flight home. As I write this, yesterday I was actually at that same stadium, photographing it for a client. If I'd been told back then that in 15 years I would be at that same stadium, taking pictures for a customer, I would have laughed. Yeah, *right!*

Little did I know, although only making a fraction of that salary, I could be infinitely happier. As Deepak Chopra says, "The Spirit doesn't see any difference between a penny and a billion dollars, it gives according to the need that must be filled."[3] I was wealthy in money and poor in everything else. Now, Spirit's abundance fills my life, and I have true wealth. But that's getting ahead of my story.

• • •

Amber and I met at MSU during my fourth year. We dated almost two years, including the eight months we spent in California. After I signed the contract with the Packers on September 5, 1989, we moved to Green Bay and continued daily drinking and drugging.

---

[3] Chopra, Deepak. *Fire in the Heart*. December 26, 2006.

Our drinking and doing recreational drugs had begun at MSU. We never had time together when we were sober until we both went into treatment. As a result, I don't think we knew each other very well.

With a $4.4 million contract, we had a lot of discretionary money, and neither of us was prepared for all that cash. We experienced a major psychological shift. For the first time in our lives, we weren't living from one day to the next. Neither of us came from a wealthy family, so when we had thousands of dollars at our disposal, we didn't understand how to budget and plan for the use of our income. We now had *opportunity* that we'd never lived with, and we didn't know how to handle it well. Of course, we spent most of it on drugs and booze. By the time we finally got sober, there wasn't much money left. That was another devastating byproduct of the control this disease had over my life.

Amber did her own thing during the day when I was at practice or training in the gym. In the spring following our move to Green Bay, she showed up at camp practice one day. That was unusual for her and I wondered why she was there. As we walked out of the gate together, she said she had to talk with me.

Something's up, I thought. But she didn't look upset or worried.

She was pregnant.

We talked briefly on our way home that day, and we agreed we needed some time to think about what we wanted to do. My tunnel-vision investment in football never allowed me to think much about being a parent. I didn't know whether or not I wanted to be a father, and had no idea if I could even do it very well, but it was too late for those thoughts. The baby was already on the way. Even though I considered not getting married, I was born and raised Roman Catholic, and marrying the mother of my child was the morally *right* thing to do.

About a month later, Amber was out for the evening and arrived home late. I had a card waiting for her on the nightstand, asking her to marry me. We both had stars in our eyes, and believed we were in love with each other. Although she wasn't my first love, I really believed I loved her; she was (and still is) a pretty woman with a caring personality. She said yes and we set the wedding date, October 19, 1990.

Our addictions didn't recognize sacred vows and solemnity. On our wedding day, ten minutes before we said our vows, I was in the basement of the church, in a bathroom stall, shooting Stadol into my veins. Once finished, I was as high as a kite. I leapt up the stairs, three at a time, and watched Amber walk down the aisle. I don't know if she got her fix or not; she had bridesmaids to contend with.

The power of chemical addiction is *unbelievable*. There we were, taking sacred vows, pledging to live a married life together, before God... and shooting that venom into our veins.

Four Years of Hell

My years of hell got dramatically worse when John revealed his diagnosis to me. I was still playing for Green Bay; it was the third year of my four-year contract. John and I hadn't spoken for two years because of a falling out we had. I felt he was jealous of my success. We both had dreams of playing in the NFL—together, if possible. He played in the CFL; but never made the NFL. We weren't talking. He was hurt, and I didn't handle his hurt well, so I just didn't talk to him for two years—and I was too loaded with chemicals to care.

When Amber and I were making plans to get married, I'd decided on the guys I wanted to stand up with me. The final list included John, but not as the best man. He was hurt again. He called me two days before the wedding and said he couldn't make it. So that added to the rift already existing between us. Again, there was no possibility any emotional pain could get through the wall of painkillers that surrounded me constantly.

The following year, he sent me a letter telling me he had cancer on his finger. It was extremely serious, the deadliest kind of skin cancer. He decided to have his finger amputated and wanted me to know. His letter cautioned me to be very careful; the percentages are very high for others in the family to have the same kind of cancer. He told me to check my body for discolored moles and anything that looked abnormal. He also provided his telephone number.

Although I didn't feel too concerned for him, his letter got through to me and I called him. We talked for the first time in two years.

"How serious is it?" I asked. I'd been thinking if he had his finger amputated, it was probably gone, so I was not worried at all.

"Pretty serious. It's the deadliest kind of skin cancer you can get." John wasn't mincing his words.

I was taken aback. I was in the midst of my drugging days and was numbed to a lot of stuff happening in my life, but I suddenly felt stunned. I couldn't imagine losing my big brother.

Then, the painkillers set in and I quickly became matter of fact about it. As real as it was, I was anesthetized enough that I didn't experience what would have had a big impact had I been sober.

I told myself, "Oh, he'll be all right." Being geographically far apart made it even easier to minimize the issue; John was in Ontario; I was in Green Bay; nothing was going to happen to either one of us.

John was dead 14 months later. The cancer was first diagnosed on his finger; six months later, he had lumps in his right elbow removed. Six months after that, further tests revealed his lymph nodes were affected, and all the treatment stopped. Two months after that, he died.

The most serious moment between John and me happened in October before he died. John came to Green Bay to see me. Cancer had gone to his elbow, but it had not manifested itself in the lymph nodes yet. He had the surgery on his elbow and then came to see me.

We spent time getting caught up with each other. He'd never seen Holly, our baby daughter. He held her and played with her a long time that day.

John was in debt to the tune of fifty or sixty thousand dollars, all on credit cards. His girlfriend was responsible for most of the charges. They weren't married, and I was never sure what their relationship meant to either of them. We didn't talk about it. I didn't know her well, but I also didn't like her.

John asked me if he could borrow $60,000 to pay off the debt. Amber and I were beginning construction on our new home, so I had a ready excuse.

I replied, "This house is expensive." Then, more honestly, "If I knew it was just you I wouldn't have a problem with a loan; but I'm not going to pay *her* bills."

We were living in Pulaski, 15 miles outside Green Bay. Our log home was quaint; the road was 1/2 mile to the corner and then 1/2 mile back to our house. John and I walked that road as we talked. We were at a dip in the road, where it went downhill; I remember the fall colors were stunning.

Ultimately, I said no and used my wife as excuse. "Amber won't go for it. I can't account for $60,000 missing. If it were just you, it'd be different."

Then, we began talking about how he was dealing with his cancer. In the middle of the road, John broke down and cried, "Tony, I'm afraid to die."

He cried in my arms in the middle of the road and I wept too. I was powerless. I could not keep my big brother alive. The $60,000 wasn't going to change the cancer. Four years before we were on top of the world; we won the Rose Bowl; his CFL team won the Canadian Championship; our parents went to both games. In four years, I laid an egg; fell on my face; didn't live up to a tenth of the expectations, and now my brother was dying. Why? Why? Why? I stood there sobbing for the tragedy in each of our lives.

There are a few major reasons why... Daily drinking and drugging make life difficult. A part of me knew that, but my ego wouldn't let me confront those issues at that time. I had a huge dilemma; I couldn't use steroids because the NFL tests randomly. I risked major salary loss if I got caught, so I stopped using steroids. Even though steroid use will always be associated with my name, it was alcohol and painkillers that stole my self-respect and success in the only game I ever wanted to play; daily use of drugs and alcohol is what almost killed me, and killed my career. It was never steroids. The differentiation doesn't justify either one, but they both played their role in a negative way.

It was my last year with the Packers. During those last two months, at Christmas time, 1992, I'd suffered a concussion in pre-season and couldn't play. I was put on the PUP list (physically unable to perform) and taken off the 53-man roster so another player could be added. I wanted to see John, and since I wasn't playing, I asked the head coach and team doctor for permission to go to Canada for a week. He granted it, so I headed to Ontario.

My biggest fear was that I'd get to Canada and be too far away from all my drug connections. *I didn't even think about my brother.* Addictions do that. The need to get the drug and take it totally overpowers every other event in the life of the abuser. My thoughts centered on the fact that I could run out of drugs. I was singularly concerned about making sure my supply lasted the entire time I was absent from Green Bay. The addiction has no room for compassion.

When I saw John, I was shocked. I wasn't sure what to expect. He'd been debating about chemo. I never asked how he looked, or whether he had decided on chemo, or if he'd lost weight. It was a touchy subject. It had always been important to both of us how athletic we looked, so I didn't ask about that during our telephone conversation. I didn't know if I was going to see a frail body or the John I remembered. Before he got cancer, he was 6'4", 290, big and strong.

John was still 6'4", but 320. He was fat and heavy. He couldn't work out anymore and he looked bloated, probably from morphine. I was stunned and couldn't believe what I saw.

He was being treated at Joseph Brandt Hospital in Burlington, Ontario. I went to his room—he was in and out of consciousness. The IV was dripping. He was terminal at this point so the morphine was only limited to the extent that he couldn't overdose and kill himself. He could get as much as he needed for pain; it was a quality of life issue. As he was lying in bed I walked in the room and saw him. He was out of it from the morphine.

The nurse gently nudged him, "John, your brother is here. Wake up now and talk with him."

Alcoholism and drug addiction take no prisoners and only permit tunnel vision. Six weeks before he died, John was lying in a hospital bed, still semi-conscious. I thought, "You lucky SOB; you get all the morphine you want." I wondered if I could get that needle out of his arm, put it in mine, hit the button five or six times, pull it out and put it back in his arm before the nurses came back. Those were my first thoughts when I saw my brother. He was dying, but I was the one who was sick.

Eventually John woke up. He wasn't sure how long they would keep him in the hospital. He was hospitalized for a three-day period for some reason I don't remember any longer. He said he could get a three-hour leave, so he would shower and we'd go out and grab something to eat.

John loved eating at Harvey's®. We went there that night and the memories I hold from those moments will always be close to me. I still cannot talk about that night without tears. I choose not to talk about our conversations; they were John's and mine, and will remain ours. We talked about the most important times in our lives, people whom we cared about and reminded each other of our childhood secrets. I can still remember almost every word we uttered.

I took John back to the hospital that night and saw him again the next morning. Morphine (John's) and painkillers (mine) clouded our conversation. And then… more memories and more tears. We hung out for two or three days. We didn't do anything, just hung out and were together, like when we were children. That was the last time I saw John alive.

I conned John's doctor out of 100 Valium. I was running low and needed reinforcements. I pled, "I forgot my pills; my back is killing me; I've got a head injury that keeps me from playing."

The physician bought my conning sob story and said, "Sure, here. Take this to the pharmacy." Drug laws are considerably stricter in Canada. A class three narcotic is hard to get. But if you know how to con, you can get it, and I was the expert con artist. By this time I had been conning people for years.

I needed something to dull the emotional pain I was experiencing, and the Valium did the job. I had to get back to Green Bay, so I kidded myself. Denial: he won't die. Hope: he'll pull through. I headed back to Green Bay, and my painkillers and booze.

Amber and I were doing lots of painkillers, and we needed to keep the supply lines open. We had moved back to Michigan in January of 1993; on February 8, 1993, I awoke at 3 a.m., hopped in my pickup and drove 400 miles from Traverse City to Green Bay. It took seven or eight hours, depending on how fast I was able to drive and not get caught speeding. I was doing what I considered most important, and that was driving the 400 miles to Green Bay to get pharmaceutical drugs from my pharmacy connection, and driving 400 miles back in one day. The pharmacy opened at 8 or 9 a.m.; I got my script that was already called in and then made the long drive back.

On that fateful drive, I stopped at a gas station, called Amber to be sure she and Holly were okay, and filled my truck up with diesel fuel.

"Hey. How are things? Is Holly okay?"

Amber reassured me, "Everything's fine. When will you be home?" Her tone of voice said something was wrong. I thought it was Amber needing her painkillers, too, and needing me to get home so she could re-stock her supply. She revealed nothing on the telephone, but when I got back home that afternoon, Amber met me at the door.

"Your dad called. John died this morning." She had known when we'd talked on the phone earlier, but didn't tell me. She didn't want me learning about John's death while I was driving. So when I walked in the house, her parents were there and she told me my mom and dad wanted me to call.

Calling my parents was tough. Both Mom and Dad knew something was wrong with me, but they didn't know what. That day is a good example of how powerful the disease is. I should have been with my brother, holding him in my arms as he died. But it was more important for me to be 1000 miles away, driving 16 hours to get 100 pills. *If you die on my time, I'll make it fit in my schedule.* That was not a proud moment in my life. One part of me felt that pain, but the addicted me didn't care because I needed to look after my addiction first.

The funeral remains blurry; I medicated myself heavily. My speech was slurry. I didn't want alcohol on my breath, so I used painkillers. It was difficult for me because Mom and Dad were devastated; they had just lost their second child. I had no one to rely on emotionally. I'm sure there were offers for my emotional support, but because of my state of mind, I held myself at arm's length.

As soon as the burial was over, Amber and I left. My parents were hurt by our quick departure; they wanted me to be with them; but my supply was running low and I had to get back. If I didn't get back and get to my connection, I'd be hurting. *Damn this disease! I couldn't even be with my parents when they needed me most.*

In the end, John died at 31 from skin cancer. At least, that was the diagnosis and that is what his death certificate says. I don't believe he died from steroids or painkillers, but I do believe all those years of chemical use didn't help. I believe his lifestyle had a lot to do with cancer; I believe his immune system was compromised.

The Milwaukee Sentinel stated in their February 10, 1993 edition, "He [John] had one of those magnetic personalities," said linebacker Patrick Wayne, a close friend and former teammate with the Riders. "He brought a great atmosphere to any team he was on."[4] But his effect on people wasn't limited to football circles. At the federal penitentiary in Kingston, Ontario, he's fondly remembered.

> "'He was one of the most popular guys to come here, said Brad Ireland, the program development director at the prison Mandarich visited twice while with the Riders. 'He didn't seem nervous in front of the guys. He joked with the inmates, talked to them, ate at their tables.'

---

[4] *Milwaukee Sentinel.* "Mandarich's Brother Dies of Cancer." February 10, 1993.

"'He told me after he was here, he just couldn't believe some of these guys were in for such heinous crimes. He saw a human side to them.'"[5] My brother's personality and love of life itself never changed.

•   •   •

During an exhibition game in Kansas City on August 8, 1992, I suffered a severe concussion. Shortly after that game, the team doctor discovered a thyroid dysfunction. I tried to practice but became ill and had to stop. The team docs thought I had post-concussion syndrome and sent me to the Cleveland Clinic.

Tests there in mid-October confirmed post-concussion syndrome. I had memory problems and residual issues from the concussion. And I was still mainlining several times a day.

Milwaukee Journal staff writer Bob McGinn wrote on October 27, 1992, "Tackle Tony Mandarich will be examined this week at the Mayo Clinic as the Green Bay Packers seek a final evaluation of his troubling physical condition."[6] Coach Mike Holmgren wanted me to go to the Mayo Clinic to try to find a treatment that would work. The post-concussion syndrome and thyroid conditions were real, but so was my daily drug abuse. I'm still amazed that no one confronted me in Cleveland or at the Mayo Clinic about the amount of drugs that *had* to have shown up in my blood work. There was absolutely no reason I should have high levels of Stadol in my system.

On September 28, 1992, *Sports Illustrated* ran the 'Incredible Bust' article. The initial call that I received from SI was totally misleading. The reporter said she wanted to interview me about my development as a player, suggesting it would be a historical review beginning with my early days in East Lansing. My friends in the Packers' organization came to my defense when the story was printed.

---

[5] IBID.

[6] McGinn, Bob. *Milwaukee Journal.* Answer Sought at Mayo." October 27, 1992.

Ron Hallstrom, one of my teammates, said, "As far as I'm concerned, that article was bull."[7] The article supposedly interviewed two unnamed ex-Packers who said I'd discussed my steroid use with them. Ron was quoted in the *Detroit Free Press* article saying he didn't know who said those things. My friend, Ken Ruettgers, the starting left tackle, said, "I think some people just like to kick a guy when he's down."[8] Even though a lot of that 'bust' article was accurate, I felt the emotional swift kick in my gut that I believe *Sports Illustrated* intended when they published it. It was 12 years before I agreed to do another interview with that magazine. Ken was right. They kicked me when I was down, and surrounded me like a pack of angry dogs, snarling and ready for the kill. They just wanted a sensational story. The article didn't even begin to approach the reality of my drug-addicted life.

In October of 1992, I was down to 283 pounds and simply not able to play football anymore. After I'd been put on the PUP list and the season ended, my contract was up. I knew team officials renegotiated mid-contract when they wanted a player to stay. Both sides agree to terms and money before the player thinks he deserves more than the team owner wants to pay; the commitment from the owner becomes the driving force and the contract provides security for the player. I didn't get any of that. I just kept mainlining and drinking and didn't care. By this time my original goal was attained, I was in the NFL. The only thing that mattered now was where I was going to get my next stash of drugs.

The *Green Bay Press Gazette* ran an article on November 13, 1992 quoting another unnamed Packers source saying my career was over. Dr. Novotny, the Packers' team physician, said that was "very premature."[9] I was suffering from severe post concussion syndrome. In reality, although the doctor had no way of knowing, I had no

---

[7] Howard, Johnette. *Detroit Free Press*. "Ill Feelings Mystify Mandarich." October 30, 1992.

[8] IBID.

[9] Havel, Chris. *Green Bay Press-Gazette*. "Second Opinion Backs Up the First." November 14, 1992.

ability to fight the residual concussion problems because of all the drugs I was taking. The reporter, Chris Havel, wrote, "Mandarich looked much the same as he did when the team granted him a medical leave of absence about five weeks ago. In that time, he has not visited the Packers' practice facility. His pallor was better than it had been in early September and his weight appeared to be in the 280s, down from his playing weight of 303 but not strikingly diminished."[10] In the final weeks with the Packers' organization, my weight fell to 260. Skinny and gaunt, I was coming off the concussion and intestinal infection I had picked up while hunting prior to the 1992 season, and drinking and drugging myself to an early grave. I convinced myself God intended me to be an alcoholic, and I just kept living up to the expectation.

The hole I dug was deep and bottomless. Media hype and Tony-hype talked about how great I was going to be. Then I didn't perform, and I embarrassed the Packers and myself; I knew there wasn't going to be any contract, mid-term or otherwise. I still didn't want to admit it, though, because my arrogant ego would not permit defeat.

Coach Holmgren continued to create opportunities for me to recover and get my strength and agility back, but I was too numbed from drugs to be able to accept those offers.

So as the end of my contract approached, Amber and I decided to move to Traverse City, Michigan for good as soon as the season was over. After Christmas, we put the house on the market. It was modest and sold quickly. Sportswriters Sharon Raboin (Green Bay Press Gazette) and Bob McGinn (Milwaukee Journal) both marked our departure with articles about selling our home near Pulaski, and my disappearing from the football scene with suggestions that I just got tired of football and my heart wasn't in it anymore. They had no idea how close to death I walked.

Amber and I moved into a rental house in Traverse City, but had such tunnel vision about drugs that we didn't do anything about

---

[10] IBID.

building on the 125 acres we owned. We knew we wanted a log home, architectural drawings were completed, but drugs were more important at the moment. After John's death on February 8th, the Packers' General Manager called me and gave official notice of the death of my NFL contract. They weren't going to renew. I was a free, drug-addicted agent.

Tom Mulhern, staff writer for the Packer Press, was the only sportswriter who asked the million-dollar question. He posited, "What nobody has completely explained is what the weight loss has to do with post-concussion syndrome. The thyroid condition was being effectively controlled by medication, Mandarich said earlier this season. But no explanation regarding the weight loss.

"The answer, of course, lies in Mandarich's deep, dark past and the allegations of steroid use that have hovered over him since his senior year of college at Michigan State."[11] Nobody who might have intervened asked me that 'why' question. And even Mulhern guessed wrong. It wasn't steroid use. It was addiction to alcohol and pain killing drugs, plain and simple, but I wasn't about to admit to my dirty little secret.

Amber and I left Green Bay. We lived off savings from the Packers contract. I didn't work. We completed the log home, conned doctors and chased drugs for the next three years.

After my physician-friend cut off my primary pipeline to legal pharmaceuticals, I scrambled for another source. I only had six connections left when I found a nurse who had access to samples. She provided me those samples, and a physician wrote prescriptions. I hated going in to his office, so I called and talked with the secretary. My con still worked. I always gave her an excuse for having to get the prescription filled earlier than legally permitted. Fiorinal #3 contained codeine, barbiturates and caffeine; it was the legal counterpart of street speedballs and infinitely safer. Percodan

---

[11] Mulhern, Tom. *Milwaukee Journal Sentinel.* "Packer Commentary: Mandarich Saga Will Soon Be Over." January, 1993.

was really hard to get, as was Percocet. But I wasn't picky; if it was a painkiller, I wanted it.

I maintained some of my connections in Green Bay, as well as with a pharmacist in California. Often I would drive the seven hours to Green Bay and seven hours back just to get a prescription filled. I didn't care where it came from. When I couldn't lay my hands on painkillers and began to run out, I drank more. On a daily basis, I awoke to reach for the bottle always sitting on my bedside table, before I even got out of bed, and counted the number of pills remaining. I constantly needed to know how long my current supply would last, and determine how I had to ration them. But I could never control the rationing. I always started the morning thinking I had to discipline myself. *Only take four or six at a time today, and they'll last longer. Then I can get to the end of the week, Thursday or Friday, and get a prescription filled again. Then I won't have to go through withdrawal.* Most of the time, what was supposed to last me three days was gone completely by the end of the first day. I'd have my pills and morning coffee and within 15 minutes, I was flying. By noon I needed more so I'd take eight Fiorinal #3, then more and more every four hours during the day. The dose I was taking was never enough. My body, addicted to painkilling medication, always got used to the dose, and then demanded more. That's the nature of drug addiction. The body acclimates to what it is given, and then insists on more to maintain satisfaction.

What the hell? What am I doing? My thoughts were there, but I was incapable of doing anything about it.

I frequented the pharmacies in Traverse City and I conned them constantly because I always needed refills before they were due. Walking in the front door sent my anxiety level soaring; I never knew whether they'd refuse or grant my refill request. At any moment they could call the prescribing doctor or the DEA and report my all-too-frequent refills. I was usually several days into withdrawal and shaking uncontrollably, both because of the DTs and because of my anxiety. I didn't know if I was facing the euphoria and relief of getting the pills again, or if I was going to hit the god-awful low of not having them for another week. I never knew until I reached the pickup window. My hands wouldn't stop shaking. If I got the pills, I wrote a check and my hands shook like those of a 90 year old with the palsy.

When a lifeline disappeared, my routine changed. I awoke to down five or six beers with three or four Fiorinal #3. That reflected my attempt to ration the pills. The alcohol in the beer intensified the effects of the drugs so I didn't need as many… until I got another supply, another lifeline. The taste of beer at 9 a.m. is bitter, but I quickly got used to it because I thought my life depended on it.

My wisdom teeth needed pulling our second summer in Traverse City. Upon completion of the procedure, the dentist gave me a script for 25 painkillers—Vicodin. Within two days, I called back reporting the pain was still killing me. So the dentist quickly gave me another prescription. That con only worked once. I couldn't get any more from him after that.

In my early days in Traverse City, I made another failed attempt to slow down my drinking and drugging. Amber and I were living in a rental house while our new log home was being built. I tried once again to wean myself off, to slow down the number of pills I took every four hours. I had a prescription for 50 Fiorinal and knew it would only last a couple of days. I knew I couldn't get any more for four or five days. I also knew my system, my body. I'd be in fiery red-hot withdrawal in 36 hours if I didn't ration them. That night I took five or six out of the bottle and took them at 7 o'clock. I had 40 left, and a brilliant idea suddenly overwhelmed me. We were building our home and storing furniture in a storage unit. *I could stash the bottle in the storage unit overnight, and then not be able to get to it because the gates would lock at 8 P.M., so I can get it back tomorrow and I will have enough to get through the next day. Delay withdrawal.* The gates wouldn't unlock until the next morning at six, and I'd have successfully rationed my remaining supply overnight. *What a brilliant idea! Why hadn't I ever thought of this before?!*

I drove to the storage facility, unlocked the front gate, and drove to our rented space. I unlocked the padlock on the door, walked in and hid the pills among the boxes and furniture, locked the padlock on the door and drove out, knowing the gates would not be open again until six in the morning. *I couldn't get to the pills until the following morning, and it stretched out the time before the DTs would set in. This is a foolproof plan!*

My brilliant idea came crashing down at midnight. I found myself at the storage facility, parking at the gate, climbing the fence to get to the only thing that mattered to me, my stash. I walked over to our storage unit, unlocked the padlock, retrieved the pills, locked the padlock, climbed back over the fence and left. I was *totally* consumed by those drugs, continuing to fall through the black hole and definitely not caring.

When autumn arrived, I hunted. But honesty compels me to quickly add that this was the only thing I did in those three years that was productive. I started dozens of projects that I never finished. Drinking and drugging were my priority, and they always interfered with doing something productive. My job, as in employment, was to always have connections active and available for prescriptions. We were still living on the money I had earned playing football at Green Bay; I was never sure when it would run out.

One of the many times I ran out of pills because my rationing plan never worked, I awoke with the telltale lower back pain. I knew my body well. Twelve hours after I ran out, I'd start hurting, and I was hurting that morning. Within just a few minutes, the withdrawal headache seized my brain in its fiery clutches. Then the sweats, those horrific sweats, began. Diarrhea soon followed, and it was impossible to get very far from the bathroom. I was lethargic and miserable and didn't want to have anything to do with anybody. *Just leave me the hell alone.* I didn't have any pills coming and wouldn't be able to get any for another week. Withdrawal is brutal. If only some pills would be coming in a day or two, I could gut it out. *Is there anyone I can call? Any lifeline I've missed?* I'd used up all of my Urgent Care cons. I'd been in all those offices too many times. They recognized me by now and knew I wasn't from out of town and didn't forget my pills.

I tried to drink beer. After the second one, the waves of nausea hit me and I barely made it to the garbage disposal side of the sink to vomit. *How many times have I gone through this? How many more times can I endure this battle before I just give up and die?* I wanted to try and get some weed and smoke it to keep me mellow, but everyone in Traverse City recognized me, and I couldn't risk getting caught and thrown in jail. It's so damn hard to even get a small package of marijuana in a small town.

Then, finally, the waiting period between filling prescriptions was over and my shaking hands gripped the bottle of 100 Fiorinal #3 once again. I'd been a week without painkillers, so I again created a rationing plan. I started with just four this time. Oh, *YES!* This time I'd make it work. I got all the way to 5 p.m. and Amber asked me about dinner. I'd just taken some Fiorinal—*How many? How many did I take this time?* I told Amber to wait a couple of hours. I wanted the buzz to kick in before I ate. I needed to enjoy the high for a while. If I had food in my stomach, I wouldn't get as high. I'd been without pills for a week and I really wanted to enjoy this.

Amber had dinner ready by 7 o'clock. We sat down to a steak dinner, my favorite. But less than an hour later, I was back at the disposal side of the sink throwing up. *How many? How many pills had I taken during the day?* I grabbed the bottle, shook out the pills and began counting. *Damn! Only 62 left!* I'd taken 38 Fiorinal #3 that day. The rationing plan failed. Again. I turned back to the sink and continued vomiting. That night, like so many others, I had to take downers to go to sleep. I'd get so high I couldn't sleep and needed chemicals for that too.

Managing drug paraphernalia challenges all abusers. I'd purchase bags of 10 1cc needles, claiming I needed diabetic supplies. Wal-Mart and local pharmacies were my suppliers. Sometimes I'd get lucky and be able to buy a full box of 10 bags. Several times pharmacists became suspicious and asked what kind of insulin I was using. My trainer forewarned me about that, and I always responded by saying I used the needles for injectable vitamin B_{12} shots for my workouts. I never re-used syringes. How strange, now that I think about it; I was willing to endanger my body every day, several times a day, injecting that poison in my system… but I wasn't willing to re-use syringes because of the potential danger of infection. That is the thinking of a true addict. We learn to rationalize everything.

So I used syringes once, broke off the tip of the needle and threw them in the drawers in the nightstands by our bed. Since I used 10-15 syringes a day, and Amber used 6-8, they collected in the drawers pretty rapidly. We couldn't throw them in the garbage because someone could discover them and get suspicious. So they piled up in the drawers.

Every month we'd clean out the drawers, after 400 or 500 needles and syringes accumulated, fill up a kitchen garbage bag and in the middle of the night, put it in a neighbor's garbage collection. My paranoia level surpassed ridiculous. After we moved to Traverse City, disposing of the needles and syringes became easier, because we lived on a farm. We had a 55-gallon burning drum, so we emptied the syringes in it and burned them. The needles were so small they were swallowed up in the ashes. We smashed the 10cc bottles of Stadol and broke them up so they weren't readable, even though our names weren't on any of those. We were very careful and expended a lot of effort to cover our tracks.

That routine continued for another two years. I was usually watching television, and managed to get to the disposal side of the sink before I'd throw up absolutely everything in my stomach. It wasn't any big deal to me, because I did that every night. It was worth the high. Day after day after day, I never got enough.

That was It and *It* wasn't good. The three years in Traverse City were the most dark and haunting years of my life. I have little memory of those days. My brain was anesthetized so much of the time that I now cannot retrieve data. The brain just cannot store it when it's so chemically altered. I regret losing those three years not only because of the drinking and drugging, but also because those were three years of Holly's life, and I wasn't there for her as I now know a father needs to be. I can never go back and give that to her. Some days the despair really threatens to consume me. I let so many people down, and most of all Holly, at such a vulnerable time. Somehow we managed to take care of her. I don't know how we did it; I don't remember much. Then I come to a moment when I become reassured... we must have done *something* right, because she is a beautiful young woman today with a sparkle in her eyes.

One of the darkest moments in my life occurred one cold December night. Amber prepared a steak for me. We'd been arguing, part of our daily ritual by that time. She knew my steak had to be well done and she was as furious with me as I was with her, slamming pans and doors in the kitchen as she prepared dinner.

After angrily dropping the steak on the coffee table in front of me, Amber returned to the kitchen. I cut into the steak and it dripped red blood. It was rare. A shock of fury, chemically powered, raced through me. I picked up the plate and slammed it into the stone fireplace wall. Our Golden Retriever, Lucky, startled and watching me carefully, saw the sirloin hit the wall. He took a flying leap, grabbed the meat in his mouth and wiped out the sirloin in three bites. A tense moment was, briefly, almost funny. I held back a chuckle watching Lucky devour the steak. But then, the fury returned with a vengeance. The dog had just eaten *my* steak. I have no memory of what I shouted, but rage consumed me and I was verbally and physically out of control.

After I'd spewed and fumed for several minutes, I turned and saw Holly standing nearby. Her eyes were full of unshed tears. She was shaking and scared to death. She didn't know what to do; didn't know if she could figure out what she could do that wouldn't provoke more rage from me. My anger and hostility instantly turned to grief as I quickly picked her up and comforted her, thinking through the clouds in my brain, *"What in hell am I doing? What in the Hell have I just done to Holly?"* She finally broke into uncontrollable sobs in my arms and I grieved with her, weeping into the dark hours of the night.

The Jumping Off Place

Numb and blurry, I chased the next prescription. I'd done absolutely nothing else for three years, and there was no reason to change the routine. I couldn't have done it if I'd wanted to—and I didn't want to.

One morning, without warning, John Whyte appeared on my doorstep. I couldn't figure out what he was doing there. John was a mentor and friend of mine, a man I'd gotten acquainted with while working out in the gym. He was an architect/builder and I had a lot of respect for him and his advice. I grabbed a couple of beers and gave him one. But why was he there? We worked out together, but we really didn't socialize outside the gym.

Then I remembered; Amber and I fought without mercy the previous night and she left with Holly, seeking refuge at her mother's. John was talking to me, but I was having a hard time following him. In the midst of the clouds and lack of focus in my brain, I suddenly and clearly heard John Whyte ask the question, *"Do you want to live the rest of your life like the last three years?"*

John's words were the proverbial baseball bat, lifted and smacked across the side of my head. Shock and disbelief overpowered everything else in my body. I was stunned, and in total disbelief. Three years had disappeared since I retired from football. Evaporated. It seemed like only three months ago. I left Green Bay in December 1992 and now it was March 1995. *What happened to my life? Where did the time go?*

Amber had called John and told him everything that was going on, so he had come out to talk to me. I resisted at first, knowing

Amber called him and tattled. That pissed me off; you don't share our dirty little secrets with anyone.

"Yeah, but I want to talk to you anyway," he said. He was a good friend, so I agreed.

Then he picked up that verbal bat and slammed it across the side of my head.

He said, "You gotta change your lifestyle, Tony. You *can't* be drinking and drugging like this." He had my attention; he'd gotten through the fog in my brain and he sounded profound. I was ready to hear it. His concern and love for me were very powerful.

"If you don't do something, the next three years of your life will go by like the last three years since you played football." I still couldn't believe what I was hearing, but he was getting through. I think I heard him because *it was finally the right time.* I was ready. I was sick and tired of being sick and tired. Tired of chasing doctors, nurses, pharmacists, arguing with Amber about how many pills we had left, tired of everything around me and mostly tired of myself. I knew in my heart of hearts that my problem was drugs. If I took that equation out of my life, everything wouldn't be rosy, but it would be a hell of a lot better than it had been. But I just couldn't stop.

I'd tried dozens of times on my own. I even went to a psychiatrist who recommended Alcoholics Anonymous and Narcotics Anonymous. He prescribed antidepressants. I never went to either AA or NA. I took the antidepressants, but they didn't get me high, so I quit taking them. Then I stopped seeing the doctor because in my mind it was just a waste of money. I was lying at $200 a session and I knew I wasn't going to take him seriously. I wasn't going to do what he said, even though he made a lot of sense. Drugs had control of my life and I wasn't going to change that. I knew I couldn't fight them and win, so why bother?

One afternoon, I found myself sitting in that psychiatrist's corner office on the fifth floor of a downtown building in Traverse City. Traverse Bay is just outside his window and the view was spectacular. I could see a shopping plaza through the other window. As we were talking, I looked out the window toward the plaza and saw the pharmacy where, after I left his office, I was going to get the next bottle of pills. I pretended to be paying attention to him. I thought, "*I wonder if he knows what kind of car I drive? If he sees my car, he'll know I'm going in that drug store. But he doesn't know why; I could be going in for razors or hand cream. He doesn't know I'm going in to get my pills. But then, who cares if he knows? I don't owe him anything.*" I realized that as far as I was concerned, seeing that therapist was a total waste of my money and our time.

That fateful morning, however, John's comments propelled me into the reality I'd successfully avoided for years. Friends and acquaintances tried to tell me I had a problem. They suggested I get help. My response? *I don't have any problems. Get out of my way.* Dozens of times over the years I gave the same response to anyone that remotely suggested I get help. One of my Green Bay Packer teammates even suggested I go to church with him, be reborn so I can see the light. I made excuses. *I have my own religion and beliefs. No thanks.* What a bunch of bull; I didn't have a problem.

Finally, I heard John. I believe teachers are sent when students are ready. I was bone-tired of myself, despised everything about me and at that moment I was willing to change. I was so tired of everything in my life going wrong. Laziness, projects I started and didn't finish, my parents, my wife... absolutely everything. I could only see my shortcomings. I had no hope, and life was grim and dark and hopeless. I'd been bulletproof for seven years, not wanting to stop drinking and drugging. *This time I wanted to stop. I heard John and I was ready to change my life. I was at the bottom of the hellhole. I had spiraled down to a place where I had two choices: either stay in the hellhole or do something about it.*

Substance abuse therapists and experts alike tell us the abuser has to come to this point in life before change can occur. We have to be willing to look at ourselves in the mirror and say, "You are a drunk/drug addict. You have no power over the drugs and alcohol you consume." Not until abusers reach this point do they have any chance of stopping the abuse and changing their lives. The offending chemicals *must* be removed, *totally*.

I finally reached that point. I was a drunk. I was a drug addict. I had absolutely zero power over those chemicals in my body and my life. They brought my life to total ruination. And now, I'd lost three years; I had, categorically, no idea where the last three years went.

I told John, "I want to stop but I don't know how. I've tried and I'm tired. A year ago I went 12 days without pills. I chose to stop and did it by pure will. I even had the pills in the house and didn't take them. After 12 days, I thought I obviously did not have an issue with drugs, because I just went 12 days without them and they were here and available. I was sure I did not have a problem, so I started using again."

The disease is so cunning, powerful and patient! This conversation with my addiction became daily dialogue in a bad neighborhood in my head. The disease always won, and now I knew it.

I continued, "So I went back at it, slowly building up over a couple of months, and back to 50-60 pills a day. How did I get here again? I don't know how to stop!"

John talked with me about treatment in a hospital. He was a spiritual man and very levelheaded. I respected him. He told me I was so seriously addicted that I needed inpatient hospitalization to dry out and then to figure out how to live without chemicals. I believed him, because absolutely nothing else had ever worked for me.

I told John I needed 24 hours to think about it and talk with Amber. When I called her at her mother's home, I reported my conversation with John. She asked if I wanted to go to treatment.

I replied, "Only if you go too. I can't go through treatment and come back here if you're still using." She didn't have to think about it for as long as I did. She agreed to go too. She was probably as tired as I was of all the drinking and drugging. In addition, she had to put up with my constantly ill-tempered behavior—not an easy task for anyone. Neither of us was a saint, but she has to get a lot of credit for hanging in with me and knowing, without hesitation, that we needed help.

We told John of our decisions and he helped with arrangements. I chose Brighton Hospital Chemical Dependency and Mental Health Residential Treatment Center; it was closest; Amber went another 30 miles on to Henry Ford Hospital in Detroit. John was at our home, with Holly and Amber's mother, when we left for the four-hour drive to the two hospitals we had chosen. They stayed with Holly to keep life as stable as possible for her. Holly had never been away from us; she was only four years old.

Amber and I drove to Brighton in my pickup. At that point, I was as desperate to change as I'd been to chase drugs, but I didn't know what the change was about. I just knew I'd try anything to live and feel differently. We left Traverse City on State Highway 72, south to I-75.

A few miles outside Traverse City, I turned to Amber and said, "Listen. I'm taking this very seriously. I'm going to the treatment center for 12 or 21 or 28 days, however long it takes, but I'm not doing any of that AA shit. I'm not going to those stupid meetings. I'll go down there and get fixed, cleaned up properly and then won't use anymore." Amber naively agreed. If she knew what treatment was all about, she didn't let on.

I believed that by the time we left treatment, our heads would be clear and we would understand why and how we could stop drugging. I knew I was a drug addict, but I also knew I didn't have any problem with drinking. At that point I believed my only problem was pills, not alcohol. To me an alcoholic was a guy with two overcoats on in the middle of summer, sitting in an alley with a bottle in a brown paper bag. I had no idea treatment was only the tip of the Disease Iceberg.

We had a prescription for a bottle of 100 pills filled the previous day. The intake workers at the hospitals where we'd registered told us to keep taking whatever we'd been taking, and not to stop. Detox would be done in the safety of the treatment center. I didn't listen to the warning in that advice. I always thought I knew almost everything there was to know in the world; I didn't even think about what lay ahead of me at the hospital. After all, I was 29 years old and had already achieved a lifetime goal of becoming a NFL player. I knew it all and nobody was going to tell me anything different.

We arrived at Brighton Hospital, where I had registered for treatment, about 9 o'clock. They weren't expecting us until 10, so we stopped at Big Boy® for breakfast. The bottle of 100 pills was down to 80 by that time. Amber took her two and went to the bathroom to down them privately. When she returned to the table, I took the bottle into the bathroom, went into a stall, locked the door and poured eight Fiorinal #3 into my hand. As I looked at the pills in my hand, I began a conversation with them. *"These are the last ones I'm taking! I'm done! I've had enough!"* I popped them into my mouth and swallowed. They went down as smoothly as always; I never needed liquid to wash them down. Then I took that bottle of 70 pills, flipped off the cap, turned the bottle upside down and, in slow motion, watched them fall into the toilet. Because they're gelatin capsules, they started dissolving immediately. I watched the blue and yellow transform into a green jelly-like fluid and thought, *"Six days ago I would have been scrambling for them. If I'd dropped one, I would have been scrambling in the toilet water for it. Now I'm dumping 70 and it feels right. I'm done with this. What is happening to me?"*

I now know Hope had finally entered the embryo stage in my heart that day, looking at the poison in my life swirling down the toilet. My dear friend, John Whyte, told me I could conquer this addiction. I allowed entry for his hope into my life. As it started to grow within me, it became mine. It slowly became a part of my life. The pills were gone. The toilet bowl was filling with clean, clear water and my new life was beginning.

Then I reached into my pocket for the knife I kept on my key ring, and scraped the name off the prescription bottle. I scrunched up the paper, put it in the toilet and flushed again. I tossed the bottle in the garbage on the way out the door.

Amber and I didn't want to order for a while so the buzz could set in. The last buzz we'd ever have from the pills. We both wanted one last time that we would remember forever. Kind of like a memento that reminds you that you don't want to go back.

After some seven or eight minutes, I asked her, "Feel anything yet?"

"Not a thing."

"Neither do I." Our bodies seemed to ignore the chemicals, as if they knew it was the last time. I thought then that Providence had already taken over. I made a conscious decision in the restroom, telling myself I was done with the pills. The last eight Fiorinal #3 I took had no effect on my body whatsoever. I should have had the buzz after seven or eight minutes, but it wasn't happening. I believe I was starting to retake control of my life and some obscure part of my body realized that.

After waiting several more minutes, we finally ordered. The buzz never kicked in.

We went into separate treatment centers. We didn't see each other for 17 days. Our new lives had begun; we went our separate ways then, an omen of our permanent separation almost three years later.

The Slow Road Back

I entered treatment at Brighton Hospital on March 23, 1995 and my love affair with sobriety began in the following days. I've never taken another illegal drug, painkiller or chemical, nor had a drink of anything intoxicating, since that day. I didn't know that March if treatment had the answers; I only knew I didn't. I knew I had a problem and that it consumed my life.

Drinking and drugging destroyed my relationship with Amber; devastating paranoia about friends and family finding out about my drugging crippled my daily life; and my inability to play football at Green Bay annihilated my lifelong dream. *My God, what wreckage I left behind!* I'd been touted as the best offensive lineman *ever* when I left MSU. When I joined the Green Bay Packers, I shattered the iconic image created in the media. My out-of-control drinking and drugging ran roughshod over everything in my life that mattered. I had to believe treatment could only improve my life; it just couldn't get any worse. My stay at Brighton included 17 days of detox and treatment for the addictions I finally admitted to my treatment team and myself.

Physically, mentally and spiritually battered from drinking and drugging, I walked into treatment voluntarily. I'd had enough, and I was ready to make changes in my life. I didn't like the man in the mirror.

Amber went into the reception area at Brighton with me. Don Daly, a nurse practitioner, greeted us. He gave us some general information and then said, "I need to give you some statistics, not to put a downer on your experience, but just to let you know what happens to most alcoholics. Eighty per cent of people going through treatment don't stay sober. Seventy-five per cent of marriages dissolve. These are facts, and you both need to decide which group you want to be part of." It was a wake-up call for both of us. We didn't discuss it, but we both knew we were in for a huge change in our lives. Amber left and drove on to Henry Ford Hospital in Detroit.

After I signed all the paperwork, Don took me to my small room. It was a cross between a hospital and a dormitory room. In actuality, it was probably more like a hospital room with some amenities added, including a dresser and a mirror. It was cold and sterile, with a linoleum tile floor, a shower for the handicapped and no cosmetic warmth at all. It wasn't inviting; it was just functional. I unpacked the small gym bag with my clothes and toiletries; Don took my nail clippers and Q-tips. I thought that was weird; *how am I going to commit suicide with nail clippers and Q-tips?* But I didn't challenge him. I'd already decided I needed to shut up and listen for a change, after all my best thinking got me to where I was at that moment. That was one personality trait I had to surrender; I had to stifle my mouth.

The rules were simple and straightforward. Curfew was at 10 p.m., lights out at 11. Televisions were only in the lounge and they were shut off at the main switch at 10. Nail clippers and Q-tips were prohibited. Groups were mandatory. Everything was sign in and sign out. Sundays were family days, but I wasn't planning on anyone visiting me, so Amber and I arranged to talk on the pay phones on Sundays. All that seemed pretty simple to me, after all the frenetic drugging of the past seven years.

I only had roommates the first and last two days of treatment. That was okay with me, because I knew I'd need some space during the time I'd be there.

Detox was isolation… no didactics, no groups, no socializing; just being alone. Most people don't want to be around anybody during detox anyway. It's physically painful and we don't want to have to deal with people. My detox time was longer than usual because of the eight Fiorinal #3 I'd taken an hour before I arrived at

Brighton. The nurse assured me they would keep me as safe as possible as my body withdrew from the chemicals. She said they'd monitor me carefully; heart attacks, seizures and strokes are common side effects of detox and she said they would give me medications to try to prevent them from happening. Don gave me some reading material and left me alone.

Then it started—the backache first; and I knew the headache would soon follow. Within a few hours, my body screamed in angry fury for the chemicals it needed. By 10 o'clock that first night, diarrhea set in; my stomach felt like it would burst with the fiery pain that consumed me. Shocking jabs of pain in my forearms and legs felt like I was connected to an electrical charge that just kept jolting my limbs. *God, this hurts!* I couldn't get comfortable in any position, sitting or lying down or standing. Nothing worked. My body was shrieking for the drugs it had for so many years, and it didn't stop for three days. It was incredible and indefinable, cruel, tortuous pain.

Phenobarbital and sleeping pills were the only medications I accepted. The nurse offered Antabuse (disulfiram), a drug that makes you violently sick to your stomach if you drink with it. I wasn't going to be drinking, but I didn't want it anyway. I didn't need to take it. Nothing but my determination would keep me sober. I could put all the fail-safes into place, and if I wanted to do something, I'd do it. So I said no to Antabuse.

On the second day the nurse gave me a wooden tool with four round legs that I used to massage my leg and arm muscles, in a mostly futile attempt to reduce the searing fire in my limbs. My body just kept screaming for the drugs, but my spirit kept saying, "No more!" A war raged inside my body and I could do nothing to stop it. I was determined to conquer the demons in my mind and the chemicals they wanted me to take.

The cafeteria was the only place detox patients were allowed to go to; we needed isolation to get through withdrawal. I couldn't sleep and my biggest fear was being up all night with nothing to do. I sat and stared mindlessly at the walls, with the unrelenting, white-hot pain roaring through me.

On the fourth day, my body gave in and gave up. The nerve receptors finally seemed to be convinced they would not get what they wanted, so they slowly stopped screaming. Like a two-year old after a tantrum, they whimpered a little, and then went to sleep in compliance. After four days, I slowly slipped into a deep sleep.

The results of my physical exam came back and, in spite of the damage I'd created over the past seven years, I was physically okay. I hadn't suffered a heart attack, nor had I experienced any seizures. That's pretty amazing given the wreckage I'd created in my heart and my brain. No one knew what permanent damage had occurred that might show up later. Only time will provide those answers.

The Phenobarbital had taken some of the edge off the pain those first four days. I was only aware of that because of my previous futile attempts to stop drugging on my own. When I tried on my own, I always continued drinking, so my attempts were always failures. On day five, I stopped taking Phenobarbital, and then only used sleeping pills when I needed them. I knew I had to learn to live from one day to the next without chemicals, so I began trying to do that after the pain and electrically-charged muscle spasms abated.

I was relieved when I could start attending group sessions and individual counseling. The isolation had ended and my time by myself became more limited. John Whyte had told me I needed to listen to what the experts said, and that I needed to participate fully in the treatment program in order for it to work, so I did. I now desperately needed to conquer drug abuse. I had a new goal: beat the chemicals. I didn't worry about being the *best* recovered drug addict; I just wanted to recover. I wanted to live.

Initially, I had some issues with my individual counselor because she had no addictions. I didn't believe she could *really* understand how I felt because she never walked in the shoes of an addict. *How can you empathize with someone if you haven't had a similar experience?* Then, after a few days, I discovered her competency as a professionally trained counselor, and the empathy issue took a back seat. She was well trained and I respected her education and training.

I went to every group session assigned, didn't miss a single individual counseling session, went to all the didactics (where I learned about the disease and how cunning it is), and attended my first AA meeting. I believed my problem was limited to the pills, and I honestly didn't think I had a problem with drinking. I knew AA was about recovery, but I was convinced I wasn't an alcoholic. I was just a drug abuser.

I still didn't think much about going to stupid AA meetings and listening to people talk about their addictions. But I soon discovered how off base my perception was about AA and its meetings. It was another one of those bats across the side of my head. I hated those bats, yet that was the only way I could *get it*.

AA at Brighton included lots of alumni, alcoholics who went through treatment there. At my first night in an AA meeting (Day 4 of treatment), a dozen of us newcomers ventured into the large room in the basement of the hospital where meetings were held. I was so happy to be out of detox. It was terribly isolated and my only communication the first three days was with other patients in the cafeteria. They were in groups or individual counseling sessions while I was drying out. I like my own space, but that was gruesome.

So I was happy to finally have some social activity. I was also naïve about what would happen at the meeting. I knew nothing about the 12 steps of recovery and the traditions of AA, nor how the meeting would progress. I sat down in the back row next to a guy who was a huge sports fan. I had played college football in that state, and it wasn't any surprise to me that he immediately knew who I was. I wasn't crazy about him recognizing me; I didn't want the world to know I was in treatment.

"Listen," I begged. "I'd appreciate it if you didn't go around telling everybody." I didn't want to advertise my presence if I could avoid it.

"I won't say a word." He was cool.

I asked him what meetings were like.

"Just a bunch of bullshit. They read stuff and you get a token if you're new. You don't have to do any of it if you don't want to." It was obvious AA hadn't made much of an impression on him.

I wanted to keep a low profile, so I decided I'd just sit there and take it in. I would not participate. After all, I wasn't an alcoholic, so I didn't need this stuff.

"Is this your first time at Brighton?"

"No. Third." He sounded rather matter of fact about it.

I thought to myself, "*Why would I want to listen to this guy if he can't get it right?*" I politely ignored him during the meeting and the rest of my time in treatment. I didn't want to associate with people that didn't want sobriety. I had too much at stake.

The meeting began with the serenity prayer, preamble, 12 steps, traditions and tokens. Tokens are presented to people in all stages of recovery, from 24 hours or a desire to stop drinking, to decades of sobriety. Because we were in a treatment center, there were a lot of newcomers. And then a beautiful girl got up and started to hand out tokens. Her eyes sparkled; they exuded the clarity and energy of sobriety. She hugged each person who received one. *Well, shit!* I hadn't been hugged for five days and she was really pretty. Four days of detox hadn't damaged my eyesight or my brain. I walked to the front of the room, got my token and a nice big hug! I thought, "If this is what AA is about, I'm all for it". I discovered then that I didn't care what motivated me to come back; I just wanted to return to AA meetings.

I watched and listened carefully. A speaker suggested to the newcomers that, unless they had something to say that was really eating their lunch, they should just sit back and listen. I just listened. I didn't want anyone to recognize me and tell the whole world I was there. There was so much new stuff to take in that it took me several days to figure it all out. All the people in that meeting were laughing. They were happy. I wondered if they were full of shit. *Are they really using drugs and just coming here saying they weren't? How can they be so happy without being high or drunk?* I stared at them in disbelief.

I entered treatment believing the fun was over, because the fun was in the bottle. But the misery would also be over; so stopping was worth the trade-off. The misery overpowered the fun for me, and I was willing to sacrifice the fun because the misery was so devastating. If I'd been told that night that in three months, I'd laugh more and have more fun than in the past seven years, I wouldn't have believed it. I couldn't remember ever having fun without being high.

I could tell who the newcomers were that night. We had bags under our eyes. We looked beat up and worn out. Many of us were still shaking from withdrawal; we were hurting. That trembling could last for a week. The alumni were laughing and having a good time. I knew I wanted that good time, and hope grew a little nearer. It was palpable. I could *feel* it. *Just maybe it's possible that I could laugh again someday.*

The meeting was tolerable, not hokey or cheesy. I do remember thinking to myself, "*I'm in an AA meeting. What the hell am I doing here?*" My goals as a child were to grow up and play football, not to grow up and be an alcoholic and attend AA meetings for the rest of my life.

That AA meeting left a good impression. I attended four or five during the 17 days in treatment, and it was good. Someone said aftercare would mean 90 meetings in 90 days. I sat and listened, still convinced that didn't apply to me.

Group started the next day; there were eight of us with a counselor. She posed her first question, "Why do you think you were drinking?" Each member of the group replied, and then it was my turn.

"I don't have a problem with alcohol. My problem is with pills." I still didn't believe there was any connection. I planned to get the pill problem fixed and then return home and resume drinking beer with my buddies while we watched football. That was fun, and I intended to have fun.

They all laughed in my face. I was crushed and I was still convinced I wasn't an alcoholic. They didn't know what they were talking about. I just had to explain it better.

But then another guy in the group who'd been there a week longer than I spoke up, "It's the same thing. Whiskey, vodka, beer, painkillers, pills... doesn't matter. *You can't drink anymore!"*

I saw the counselor nodding in agreement. I thought to myself what a bunch of bullshit that was.

"What are you guys talking about?" I was shocked. I *couldn't* be alcoholic. I just had one problem, and it was pills. I knew that and I admitted it.

The group members explained addiction; it was totally new. They said it's all about behavior. You take a chemical from outside your body, ingest it because it will alter your behavior and make you think you feel good, all for the purpose of getting away from yourself. The chemical doesn't matter... alcohol of any kind, whiskey, beer, meth, speed, Fiorinal, Percocet, cocaine, heroin... all for the sole motivation to change the way you feel, numb the pain and get high.

Addiction, in medical terms, is the *physical* dependency on a substance, just to function normally and make it through the day. One's body physically requires the chemical to maintain homeostasis. My body physically required the painkillers and beer. Outside the medical field, the term addiction is also used to define *compulsive* behaviors, that is, a *psychological* pressure (addiction) to do something repetitively that usually has bad consequences (overeating, gambling, compulsive hand washing, etc). I may have had those too, but the physical addiction overwhelmed absolutely everything else in my life.

"So what you're telling me is I can't sit around and watch a football game and have a beer with the guys?" I needed to be sure I heard correctly.

"Yeah, that's what we're telling you." They all affirmed, nodding their heads.

I was stunned. That's the first time I heard about alcoholism and I wasn't sure I agreed, but I didn't completely resist. I went back to my room and thought about it for 24 hours. Then I started remembering... all the times I drank beer at 9 a.m. because I'd run out of pills. I remembered substituting beer for pills when I made my futile attempts to ration a dwindling supply. Over those 24 hours, reality dawned, and I understood. It was crystal clear. I wouldn't, and couldn't, be drinking anymore.

Learning about alcoholism came out of left field. I'd had no obsession about drinking beer in the first five days. I'd never thought, *"I can't wait to get out of here so I can have a beer."* Alcoholism just wasn't part of my problem. I was a drug addict. I was at peace knowing and working on that.

I revealed my newfound understanding of my addictions the next day at group. I told everyone there that I understood about alcoholism, and I was done drinking beer. Within a day or two, my body was physically hurting again. The day was horrendous. It may have been the 'last hurrah'... my sober nervous system making one last attempt to cry out for drugs. I've learned that it's not unusual, in cases of very serious and highly excessive drug abuse, for the abuser to experience another withdrawal siege after the primary course is exhausted. The second one is less intense and doesn't last as long.

Patients at Brighton represented every walk of life; politicians and priests, professional athletes and musicians, General Motors and Ford executives and employees, mothers and models, executives and blue collar workers. This disease isn't picky; it doesn't discriminate. And it's very patient. One guy, a 50 year old, had 25 years of sobriety, and was back in treatment because he relapsed. His story scared the hell out of me. He had been sober for nearly half of his life and he relapsed; I didn't know that could happen. I thought once you were sober and not using drugs, the addiction no longer existed. I was beginning to be cognizant of some very important facts; I could *never* even think about doing drugs or beer or booze of any kind, ever again, in life. I would always be in recovery. It's a never-ending condition.

Another young guy had been there a week before I arrived. I only saw him in the cafeteria, moving at one mile per hour. He didn't talk with anybody; his eyes were glassy. We all wondered what was wrong with him. Some of us guessed he'd done so many drugs that he fried his brain. His room was two doors down from mine.

As we became acquainted with each other, we'd hang out in our rooms together. I walked by his room several times, only to see him sitting on his bed staring out the window. He didn't move; he didn't do anything. I felt sorry for how messed up he appeared to be.

As I read in my room one evening, a horrible stench emanated from the hallway. I thought a sewer had backed up nearby. I ventured into the hallway slowly, and the smell worsened as I approached. The kid was in the hallway, wearing only his shorts, squatting down on the floor. He had defecated on the floor in the hallway just outside his room. As I entered the hall, he stood up and feces ran down his legs and spread over a wide area on the floor. The kid just stood there, looking around. He was a zombie; he probably didn't even know what he had done. I thought, *"That could have been me. I took so many drugs that I could have fried my brain."* I felt grateful it wasn't me, but I knew I could degenerate into that condition if I returned to drugging. I didn't say anything to him or to anyone else. Some patients didn't know what to say, so they made fun of him. I couldn't make fun of him, because that could have been me.

The Saturday night AA meeting was a big one, with over 150 people attending. It was my last AA meeting during treatment and the big room in the basement was even bigger with all the doors open to hold the large crowd. As the speaker entered, I looked at him in amazement. He was massive, having muscles coming out of muscles. He was especially interesting for me because of my interest in weightlifting and football. He gave a very compelling talk; he was a very humble man and he described part of his life that I could relate to.

He'd won national championships in bodybuilding. He talked about training hard, using steroids, painkillers, and drinking. Then one night, he returned home and lay in bed gazing at all his trophies. He felt empty inside and realized the trophies didn't mean a thing to him. They were a symbol of a theft; they'd robbed him of who he really was. He tossed all the trophies and got sober. He returned to bodybuilding, drug-free, and sober.

That guy made an impact on me. I left that meeting telling myself that if he could do it, so could I. I quietly vowed to myself to try playing football again someday.

During classes called didactics, we learned that out of the 40 of us in treatment at the same time, only one of us would never drink or drug again. Two will be sober more than five years; and then we heard more statistics about the number of people who were sober only a year, or only a month. It was chilling to look around the room and consider that most of the group would never remain sober.

My strong will and constitutional determination, inherited from my parents, emerged during didactics. I heard those percentages. The statistics further served to challenge me.

I believed there wasn't any reason I couldn't be that one who makes it, the one who never drinks or drugs again. So many things happened in my life that weren't supposed to be possible... long shots. Long shots like coming from Canada and being the second pick in the NFL draft. I thought if I could do that, why couldn't I be the one out of 40? I was in the top two out of thousands of football players. I can handle one out of 40. *I chose to be that one.*

On day 11, several of us were hanging out in the lounge. It was Sunday and no groups or didactics were scheduled. All the other patients were smoking. I didn't smoke, but I did chew tobacco. We were all telling our stories, talking about all the nonsense we'd lived through in our drinking and drugging days. We described the lengths we'd go to, to get drugs or booze. One laugh drew another and soon we were all busting our guts with laughter. The smoke finally got to me and I returned to my room. I sat down on my bed, trying to get my stomach muscles calmed down from all the laughing. *Man, I can't remember the last time I laughed that hard; my gut hurts!* From that moment on, I was hooked—the laughter hooked me! I didn't know what it was all about, but whatever *it* was, *I wanted it!* I liked the way it felt, and *It* felt good.

That moment was a major crossroads in my life. I believe, at that crossroads, I made the choice to take the sobriety path and not look back. It was the jumping off place for me. I jumped off the train determined to live differently. The AA Big Book[12] describes the importance of a jumping off place, the place where the recovering addict chooses to make life-impacting changes. The path to more drugs and drinking no longer appealed to me. The bottle and the pills no longer provided laughter, only misery. The drugs and alcohol were no longer in control and I could focus again; I could think again. I chose, consciously and intentionally, to turn away from misery and begin walking the path of sobriety. I finally experienced laughter and I *knew* how it felt; sober laughter, and I knew it was abundant on that path.

The cycle of classes, group sessions and counseling began again on Monday. I'd gone through it twice already, and because the cost of treatment was coming out of my pocket, I went in to see the doctor and told him I'd be leaving in the next few days.

He closed the door. "Tony, this disease is cunning. It will tell you you're good to go, that you've gotten on top of it. You've been drinking and drugging for years. You're only 14 days dry and sober. You've safely detoxed and you are getting educated and introduced to AA… but you're not ready to go."

He opened his desk drawer and pulled out a rubber toy monster. "This is alcoholism." He put the toy on my shoulder.

"It's on your shoulder now. Right now it's telling you you're good to go, that you've learned everything you need to learn and you can leave now. But I'm telling you that you're not ready." He was insistent that I remain in treatment.

---

[12] *AA Big Book, Fourth Edition.* (New York: Alcoholics Anonymous World Services, Inc., 2002), p. 152.

"I appreciate what you're saying. I'm not willing to go through this cycle another week. It's repetitive; we talk about the same stuff." I was equally insistent.

He said, "Okay. But I will have to say you left against medical advice (AMA) and that will be on your record. Your insurance may not cover the cost of treatment."

I reminded him, "This is coming out of my pocket. I don't have insurance coverage."

He seemed to think that made a difference, because he stopped trying to change my mind and simply wished me well.

I told him I'd leave on day 17; that was the day Amber was being discharged so we'd return to Traverse City together.

I had a final meeting with my counselor, creating a post-discharge game plan. I knew that maintenance would be with me the rest of my life. She reminded me that I needed to go to 90 AA meetings in 90 days, get a sponsor and don't go to slippery places (old hangouts and pharmacies for me).

She didn't have much of a sports background, but she knew I'd been active in sports all my life. She thought getting physically active again would help recovery. My endorphins needed a major boost. She was crystal clear about the fact that this alone would not keep me sober. I had to do regular meetings, keep working the steps to recovery and have regular talks with God. Physical exercise would just get me feeling better about myself. She pointed out its value in my life, and that made sense to me. I was listening to everyone, knowing and believing I no longer had the answers.

We created a list of do's and don'ts. I agreed to go to Intensive Outpatient treatment at the hospital in Traverse City, and she lined that up for me. I also signed on to see a counselor twice a week for three months, and then reevaluate counseling for the future. There wasn't any hammer held over my head, nothing anyone could do or say to make me follow the plan. I was paying for everything out of my own pocket. But I was as determined to stay sober as I'd been to do drugs before treatment, and that determination kept me on the right path. I felt I got what I needed in treatment, and I'd always had goals in life that I attained, so I didn't think any problems would arise. Now, maintaining my sobriety became my primary goal in life.

There were some for whom it wasn't a priority. During my 17 days in treatment I talked several times with one guy in particular. We exchanged telephone numbers, and he called me a week after I left treatment.

"So, are you going to meetings every day?" His voice sounded sarcastic.

"Yeah, I am. Every day." My plan called for 90 AA meetings in 90 days, and I was determined to do what my plan called for.

"Are you *really?*" He sounded incredulous.

"Aren't you?" I didn't hide my astonishment. Why in the world would anybody want to go through treatment and not follow the plan?

"Well, I've gone to a couple meetings." He didn't sound convincing. And then he asked, "Are you staying sober?"

"Yeah. I haven't had anything to drink and I haven't done any drugs. What about you?" I wasn't sure I wanted to hear his response.

"Well, I've had a few beers, but it's no big deal." I knew then he'd be part of the 80% who go through treatment, don't commit to a maintenance program for the rest of their lives, and subsequently return to their addictions.

"Hey man, just be careful; you'll end up back in treatment; please be careful." I ended the conversation. I never heard from him again. I was shocked that a week later he was drinking again; he was so sincere in the group. He talked about how he'd stopped drinking and partying, how he intended to show up for work on time and treat his employer with respect. It was all a big con. He conned us all, but I realized that he conned himself most of all.

Once beyond my initial reservations about my counselor, we began to talk about my issues. As I began to take inventory of my life, a sense of grief overwhelmed me. *I'd hurt my family so deeply.* I wasn't a good dad to Holly. My rage had free reign almost daily, and Holly was usually around to watch. She had to be terrified of me. Damage I'd created in Holly's life was at the top of my grief list.

Writing a personal inventory is Step 4 of the recovery plan. My inventory included a list of the people I wronged. I talked about those wrongs with my counselor, and she helped prepare me for making amends with them. She had no way of knowing how the scenario would play out as we talked about it. She emphasized the same thing my sponsor did later on, and that was that amends are made because *I* need to make them; I couldn't count on a pre-programmed response from anyone on my list. I had to do this for me. So I wrote a letter to each member of my family; I made copies so I would never forget what I had done, and what I hoped I would never do again.

Making amends is a structured way of telling someone you were wrong for the way you treated them. The structured part of it is important, because you need to tell them what you did that you are sorry for, and you have to accept responsibility for your actions. It's an important part of the recovery process and I'm convinced that it helps the abuser face the reality of the emotional damage he/she created for loved ones. When you know how deeply you've hurt someone, and you know you can never 'take back' the action, the vow never to do that again is easier to keep.

My hospital counselor wanted me to go through the first five steps while at Brighton. Recovery steps are in sequence for a reason and I needed to complete them under her guidance. The steps are just that, steps that must be completed before the abuser is ready to go on to the next level; they build on each other and the result is a solid foundation for life if the steps are followed.

When I admitted my life was unmanageable because of drugs, a new awakening began for me. That happened before treatment, on the day I made the decision to go to treatment. Then on day five, I had admitted my alcohol addiction and added that to the unmanageable list.

I'd always remained spiritual at heart, probably because of my strict Roman Catholic upbringing. It wasn't difficult for me to recognize God's power to restore me to sanity. Step two was just admitting what I've always known, that God is all-powerful. That has always been reassuring for me.

Step three requires that an addict turn his will and his life over to the care of God. I have to keep God in my life to keep the chemicals at bay; I can't do that by myself so I have to turn that over to God. He's in charge of my life; I'm not. After having a chance to reflect, I realized that actually happened to me in the bathroom in the restaurant when I dumped pills into the toilet and watched them disappear down the drain. I didn't know any of the steps at the time, but a year later I was in a step study group. We were talking about making a conscious decision to turn life and will over to God. Upon reflection, I remembered thinking it was *my* will power that dumped the pills, but in the study group I realized it wasn't. That simple act was much more profound. Drugs and alcohol would no longer control my life; God was in charge from that moment on.

After I wrote my personal inventory, I needed to share it with someone else, with God and with myself. My inventory was brief at the time. Nowadays I add to it when I know I've hurt someone and need to admit it and make amends. Then I wrote about how I lied, hurt my family, wasn't a good father and husband, wronged a lot of people and gossiped. I was only 15 days dry when I wrote it, not really sober yet and certainly not understanding the magnitude of life changes ahead of me. As I talked about the fifth step with my counselor, she recognized the grief I was experiencing. Ultimately, she said I was losing my best friends: pills and beer. She was right, and I was ready to find human replacements for them.

My counselor told me to do steps four and five again with my sponsor, after I'd been out of treatment and dry for a while. She said I could get more specific then, and she was right. Five months later, I did another inventory and shared it with my sponsor in Traverse City. It was much more involved and complete.

The staff said to everybody, "Do *these simple things and you will stay sober.* Change all those bad habits, including where you hang out and what you do on Sundays. Do the right things; you know what they are. If you've been going to the bar and drinking and watching football, your best bet is to NOT go to the bar. It's a slippery place."

I didn't have a better or worse chance than anyone else. I was a drunk and a drug addict. Everybody in treatment at Brighton had the same issues. Mine were just lived on the front page of the paper for the whole world to see. But we all felt the same pain, isolation, and anger. I didn't have it any easier or any harder. Some patients suggested to me that since I had money, it was easier for me to be sober. In reality, I can make the same argument for relapsing into drugging again; i.e., it's harder to stay sober because I have the money to buy drugs. It all just comes down to making a choice.

I left Brighton in mid-April, still physically, mentally, emotionally and spiritually beaten up. My skin was a sick shade of yellow and the whites of my eyes were yellow, too. My eyes were sunken in, surrounded by dark rings. I'd lost 20 pounds, and weighed only 255. I looked in the mirror in my room before I left and saw a meek, beaten-up man with his tail between his legs.

Amber left Henry Ford on the same day, picked me up, and we returned to Traverse City together. As we drove up to our log home, Holly ran out to greet us. We were ecstatic to see her! The separation was long for all three of us; both Amber and I adored our little girl. John Whyte and Amber's mother were there and welcomed us warmly. We wanted some time with Holly, so we headed off to Pizza Hut for some lunch. That was about the best kid-friendly place available in Traverse City at that time. We looked at the menu and Holly described the kind of pizza she wanted. We ordered, and chatted with her, asking her questions about what she did while we were gone. She was 'Chatty-Cathy'—a highly verbal four-year old— and she described a variety of entertaining activities with her Nana and John Whyte.

The waitress brought our order. Holly looked at her pizza and announced that it wasn't what she wanted. She didn't want the pepperoni. We offered to take the round slices off the top, and that was equally unacceptable. When she realized we weren't going to order her another pizza, she proceeded to throw a no-holds-barred four-year old tantrum. Holly has excellent verbal skills, and she used absolutely every one of those skills as her tirade grew in volume and intensity. She kicked, screamed, flung her arms wildly, yelled her version of obscenities and drew the attention of every patron in the restaurant.

I couldn't believe my ears, let alone my eyes.

In the midst of her screeching, I looked at Amber and said, "Can you believe this is happening, and we're both calm?" The tantrum wasn't a new experience, but our calm and reasoned response was. I was always about yelling and screaming; being calm was different for all of us. We'd just have to get used to it.

As our embarrassment grew, I suggested, "Let's just go home." We left the uneaten pizza on the table. I picked up Holly, who was still kicking and screaming, and headed out the door, tucking her under my arm like a football. The customers' eyes were on us, probably wondering when we were going to beat the little brat bloody.

Amber and I reminded each other, "You know, this isn't the kid's fault. This is our fault. Her tantrum is a direct result of the kind of parenting we've been doing. But the great thing is that we can correct this by changing *our* behavior."

Her punishment for misbehaving was either to stand in the corner or stay in her room. She ran to her room and slammed the door. Soon, though, her rebellious nature surfaced and she refused to stay in her room. We went upstairs and calmly told her she had a choice to either stay in her room or I'd make her.

She screamed, "You can't make me!"

I calmly put her in her room and closed the door, holding the doorknob to keep it shut. Amber came upstairs with our AA Big Book; she sat down with me and we started reading. She read a couple of pages, and then I read a couple. Holly lay on the floor on the other side of the closed door, kicking it ferociously. I thought she'd bust it, she kicked so hard. She just wouldn't give up.

The experience was new for all of us. We weren't angry with Holly; her reaction was our fault. The rules suddenly changed and she didn't know what to do. And as any four-year old will tell you—when in doubt, throw a tantrum. She couldn't change overnight, because she didn't get to this place overnight.

In the middle of our reading the third chapter, Holly wore herself out. We opened the door when her kicking stopped. She had passed out, having cried herself to sleep. She awoke as we picked her up to hold her. We began talking about what was different. Our lives were going to be different and we'd have some head butting sometimes, but things would get better. It took time, but our lives did get better, and slowly the head butting eased up.

Amber and I had only been sober around each other the first year we met. Both of us were into the recreational drug scene after the first 12 months of dating. That was not enough time to get to know each other well. When we became sober, we discovered we were strangers. Don Daly, the intake counselor at Brighton, forewarned us about how treatment would change our marriage. We thought we would get to know each other when we got sober. We did, and I began to realize I wasn't in love. Amber is a great mother and a good woman, and she was a much better wife than I was a husband. But loving someone for who she is is different from being *in love* with that person. I had to be true to myself.

I questioned our relationship and how I honestly felt about her. I prayed about it. I wasted so many years drinking and drugging and I didn't want to waste any more time doing something I didn't want to do.

Some would say our marriage was doomed to fail, and that may be true. I'm just aware that, once sober, many things changed in my life, feelings *and* perceptions. I didn't want to make any irrational decisions. Being sober was new and I had to adjust to all that it meant.

Not knowing what else to do, I started working out in the gym again and going to AA meetings. For the first time in a *long* time, I enjoyed working out. *I really enjoyed it.* I probably looked like a maniac, in the gym six days a week. I'd been unemployable for three years. This was a whole new miraculous experience! I read, prayed, did meditations in the mornings, helped around the house and went to meetings at night. I watched football on TV and got excited about it. I was 295 pounds; strong, clean and sober. No steroids, no booze, no drugs. I slept, ate, went to meetings, worked at creating a stable emotional life and did all the right things. That was maintenance and I was determined to make it work. Finally, after all the years of drugging, grief and wreckage, my life became structured and predictable.

Mom, me, Dad and John in 1969—one of only two formal family pictures we ever had taken.

4th or 5th grade—my school pic from St. Michaels Elementary School in Oakville, Ontario (approx 1976).

On our family farm in Milton, Ontario (1979)

At a football camp in Toronto, when I was a freshman in high school. I wasn't participating—I was watching John (1980)

Taken on Press Day in 1984, as an incoming freshman at MSU. Notice how skinny I was—6'6", 270 pounds.

On the sidelines at an MSU game—notice the 'EVIL' sticker I had placed over the manufacturer's name on my helmet

Mom, me and Dad during Christmas break in 1988, in our family room in Oakville, Ontario. Notice that my parents built a 'football memorabilia' wall surrounding the fireplace!

John on the sidelines during a game in 1988. He played for the Edmonton Eskimos for 8 or 9 years.

At my personal Combine in the Michigan State University indoor practice facility (early 1989).

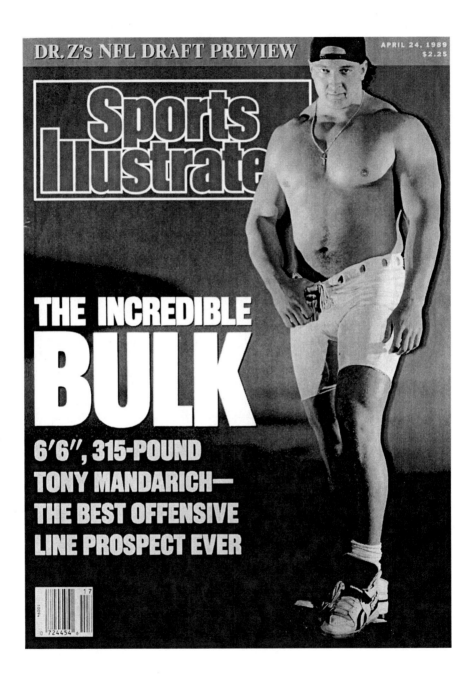

On the sidelines at a Colts game in 1998.

Tony & Sparty at the 2005 MSU vs. U of M game—Char and I had sideline passes and spent the afternoon photographing the game. It was quite a different perspective from the last time I was on that field in 1988!

Tony, Char, and our four children—Holly, Alec, Ariana and Brittney in the summer of 2006. (photo credit Paul Markow)

Making Amends

I'd hurt my parents so deeply that I questioned whether or not they could ever forgive me. After John's funeral, they needed me with them for comfort and reassurance. Two of their children had died, and I was the only one left… yet all I could think about was getting back to my comfort zone in Traverse City, since I knew my drug connections were there.

That poison was more important to me than remaining with my parents through another devastating loss. In addition to the deaths of two of their children, they then experienced the emotional loss of me. I wasn't there for them when they needed me. They were left childless at a time of unbearable pain and loss, and I had to get back to Michigan so I could be close to my pill supply. I'd made getting and doing drugs more important than my parents, and that was unforgivable.

A year after John's death, my mother had called to tell me my dad was divorcing her. Through the haze and cobwebs of my brain, I felt stunned. *My parents, divorcing? That's impossible!* We were Roman Catholic, and we just don't get divorced. Not my parents. They had been married 41 years.

I invited Mom to come spend some time with us, and she flew to Traverse City to see us. She wept, telling me the whole story. She was still grieving over John's death. She couldn't get over it, and my dad said it was time to move on. She'd tried to let go of the grief, but it continued to return and swallow her in its clutches. She felt as if she had nothing to live for, especially now that Dad was divorcing her.

I was furious with my father, and her sad tale fed that fire. She asked me to question him and his motives. My chemically induced frame of mind quickly jumped to her defense and I called my dad.

"What's going on, Dad? Why in hell are you divorcing Mom?" I didn't even try to hide my anger.

"Tony, I've had enough. We lost John last year, and your mother cannot stop grieving. I think she should let go of his death, and she won't. She's miserable every day and I've had enough." Dad's attitude was that this has happened, and now we need to let it go and get on with our lives. My mother couldn't do that, and Dad couldn't live with her daily grief.

A huge drama of gossip, innuendo, and he said/she said ensued. I was already chemically impaired, and the drama injected outrage into my fried brain. I accused my father of being a coward. I told him he needed to wake up and return to his wife, providing comfort and support for her grief. My words were harsh and my voice loud. I hurt him, crushed him emotionally. What I didn't understand was that his tolerance level was pushed to the limit by my mother. He'd really had enough. He lost his second child. I was in the States, not living at home and not visiting, consumed with a disease he knew nothing about. He tried to comfort a woman who couldn't be comforted, but found that futile and gave up.

My ties with my dad were severed for four years because of my angry outburst and accusations. From 1994 to 1997, we didn't speak. I became sober in March 1995, but it was still two and a half more years before I initiated a conversation with him. I didn't know how to make amends with him, but I knew I didn't want to do it over the telephone. I talked with my sponsor and AA friends about how to get back in touch with my dad.

Just before Christmas of 1997, I made the first attempt in four years to talk with my dad. I called to wish him a Merry Christmas. The conversation was short, but, because I was sober, I realized our estrangement was not my dad's fault; it was mine. I was the one who lashed out at him and said those awful, unpardonable things. My dad told me the divorce was none of my business, and he was right.

My parents' divorce was their business, not mine. They are both still my parents… my dad and my mom.

I was in an AA meeting, three or four years sober, and heard a guy say he wanted to make amends with his dad but put it off because he was scared. His father died suddenly, and my AA friend never got a chance to make amends. He was 11 years sober. My response? *"Oh, my God! That could be me."* I vowed I wasn't going to be in those shoes. I called my dad the next day. It was just before Christmas of 1998, and another year had gone by without seeing him. Holly, who was living with Amber after our divorce, was coming to Indianapolis to join me for the holidays. I asked Dad if we could come up and visit them. Dad said we'd be welcome.

I couldn't just say, *"I'm sorry."* I'd said that too many times. My sponsor told me how to make amends. I knew my efforts might be rejected, but I had to do this for me, not for anyone else.

We talked for four hours, and I told him I was wrong for the things I'd said to him, for the way I treated him, for not staying in touch, and for not communicating. I told him about drinking and drugging, and living selfishly in my own world. I tried to tell him I didn't do that anymore. Being mean, full of anger, loud and arrogant was what I did when I was drinking and drugging; those can still be my behaviors when I am sober, but I don't want to act like that anymore. I want to change. Part of the change was coming to him and saying I was wrong for the way I treated him.

My sponsor said my dad might not accept amends, and helped me realize that I needed to offer them anyway. I did that to take care of my side of the street. I knew the more I had wronged someone, the harder it was to make amends and for the other to accept them. I didn't relish the idea of looking my father in the eye and saying I was wrong for the way I treated him. My life depended on it, though, and I had to do it because it was the right thing to do.

Dad was surprised and taken aback by my revelations. I don't think he understood how bad my drug and alcohol addictions had been. That night at dinner, he offered me a glass of wine. He probably thought I had a drinking problem, and it was now under control, so I could drink normally. He didn't understand I would never drink again in my life, but he accepted every word I said, and he told me he loved me. He understood what I was doing and he accepted it without question. The grace in unconditional love is amazing. I still feel totally loved by my dad, although in my mind I have sometimes been undeserving of his love.

I lied to Mom about not taking drugs, but I didn't attack her like I did my father. I never had a four-year falling out with her, so making amends with her was easier. I'd done stuff she wasn't crazy about, but I knew she wouldn't reject my efforts. She asked about steroids when that hit the press, and I lied and said I didn't take them. I wasn't present for her emotionally as much as I could have been during the time of John's illness and death, and that was wrong. So I made amends with her, and she told me she always loved me and always would.

I isolated myself from my parents while I was drinking and drugging; it was easier to be away from them. I didn't want them to see my daily behavior that resulted from my addictions. If they had, they'd have known there was something wrong. They would have seen the bags under my eyes, the constant vomiting, runny nose, cold and hot sweats. They both suspected something was wrong, but they didn't know what and didn't ask much.

I tried to make amends with my brother, but, because he'd died four years previously, I never felt closure with him. I didn't need a response from him as much as I needed to know he heard me. John Whyte and I talked about it, and shortly thereafter, he offered a solution.

Five to six months into sobriety, I had developed a daily routine with John Whyte that worked well. I awoke and did prayers and meditations in the morning, followed by a workout with him at the gym. A lot of my questions about how to live a sober life were answered in the AA meetings I attended and by just being sober, but I had three big ones that remained elusive. My first question was about my spiritual guide; I wanted to know who the spiritual guide was to whom Whyte kept referring. He said spiritual guides provide help and direction in your life; you're not really aware they are there, but they are very important in leading a spiritually driven life.

The second question was a constant struggle for me: Should I play football again or not? Do I resurrect the football chapter in my life, and then close it? Or do I just leave it alone?

Should I? Could I? My big concern was about drinking and drugging again if I made a comeback. Football and drugs was the association I carried with me from my Green Bay years; one just always necessarily included the other. I decided only God had the answers to my three questions, and God wasn't talking at the moment, or maybe I wasn't listening.

The third question, and probably the most significant one for me, was about my brother. I'd written him letters trying to make amends for how badly I had treated him when he was dying. I went to the cemetery to talk with him, but that never completely quelled the desire, the need to tell him how sorry I was that I wronged him. I never felt like I'd really completed the amends.

I shared my questions with John Whyte. We talked about the elusive answers and then one day he asked if I'd like him to take me on a spiritual journey. He explained it is a Native American spiritual experience to get answers to difficult life questions. Shamans have conducted such journeys for centuries and I was excited about John's offer.

John instructed me to find a comfortable place, either sitting or laying down. I chose the bed. Not knowing what to expect, I felt tense. He started a CD with quiet, calming music. I lay on the bed with my arms stretched out by my side. John sat in a chair by the bed.

"If I ask you questions, you can nod or shake your head or answer verbally, if you want. You will be conscious and aware that you're here in your bed, but your spirit won't be here."

I didn't know what any of that meant, but I trusted John and followed his instructions.

John told me to feel the calm enter my body, breathe slowly and feel the muscles in my body relaxing, one by one. I felt my body slowly relaxing into a calm, almost ethereal place that I'd never before experienced. I was aware I was still in my bed, and the calming effects on my body felt great.

I was unaware of time, sounds or surroundings. All I know is the next thing he directed me to do was to *think* of an ideal place where I wanted to go… ideal temperature, ideal weather, ideal serenity and beauty. John didn't know where I wanted to go to; I didn't tell him, he didn't ask. The place I chose was a beach in Alaska. It was 55 degrees, dark, and ominous but at the same time serene; clouds covered the sky, beautiful crisp fall weather filled the landscape. It became so real I could even smell musty fallen leaves, sheltering the roots in preparation for the forthcoming cold winter.

"Let your spirit leave your body now. Feel it move out the top of your head… through the roof of the house… head in the direction you want to go." He spoke softly, "Ah, you're heading northwest… notice the lakes and streams in Northern Michigan below you, the beautiful green forestland. You see the people below you. Be aware of where you are. Keep traveling, and when you get to your destination, let me know."

I felt a little freaked out that he knew I was heading northwest, tensed up a little, but then immediately relaxed again when I saw the beauty of the land below me. I was moving swiftly but calmly just above the ground. I could see everything below me. Then I arrived at the beach. It was like I had envisioned. I stood on a bluff overlooking the ocean; grass under my feet stood about two feet tall. It was wet from rain, but the rain had stopped; beautiful gray cloud formations filled the autumn sky. Peace permeated the spot; it was beautiful and ideal.

In front of me lay a two-track walking path used by animals on their trek from the pasture on top of the bluff down to the beach. The two-track was lined with huge rocks.

John asked, "Look around, do you see your spiritual guide?"

The ocean was off to my right. I looked down the two-track and at the bottom of the path, on the beach, was a man sitting Indian-style facing away from me, with a bear hide around his shoulders and the bear head on top of his head.

I nodded. Goosebumps covered my body.

"Do you see the two-track in front of you?" How did John know about the path? He must have been there with me. I hadn't told him about the two-track. More chill bumps. I nodded.

"Walk down the two-track and ask your spiritual guide your questions. He knows you are here." John's voice remained soft and calm.

As I walked down the path, I prepared myself for a Native American Shaman spiritual guide; I thought in stereotypes and that notion fit the typical image of a spiritual guide.

The guide sat in front of a fire pit about three feet across. The sand on the beach was damp from an earlier rain. As I descended the path, I saw the pathway made clear by the passing of many animals on it. I walked around to face my guide.

There sat John, my brother.

I was stunned. In total shock, I began crying. I knew I was still in my bed in Traverse City, but I was also on a beach in Alaska looking at my brother. My crying turned to racking sobs.

I felt John Whyte's hand on my forearm. "Are you okay?"

I nodded yes. John Whyte sat there, his hand on my arm, until the sobs abated.

"Do you see your spiritual guide?" he asked. I nodded again.

As I slowly calmed down, breathing deeply again, John Whyte said, "Sit down in front of your spiritual guide." He had to know my spiritual guide was sitting. His instructions made sense only if he could see too.

My brother had a grin on his face. Before I descended the path, I had already manifested the Indian in my conscious mind. My stereotypes were messing with my head. It totally blew me away when I saw John.

"So you're my spiritual guide!?" I was astonished.

John nodded.

"So you know why I'm here?"

Again, he affirmed knowing what I needed. Then, finally, I made amends with John; face-to-face, knowing he heard me and knowing he accepted my sorrow. I told him I was wrong for the falling out we had and not being there when he was sick. I did a lot of things that were wrong and I told him what they were.

John nodded.

"You know that I'm sober now. This is something I have to do. I did so many things wrong the last four years of your life."

My brother accepted my amends and forgave me. He was so gentle and serene, showing understanding and compassion.

My tears finally stopped and I posed the final question, "Should I go back and play football?" I didn't go into any reasons or concerns or conditions. I just needed to know, yes or no.

John looked at me. He looked at the fire when I talked or asked a question, and then he looked at me when he spoke. He grinned and said, "I think you know the answer to that!"

"That's your answer?" I was astonished. "Couldn't you just say 'yes' or 'no'?" It was the shittiest response he could have offered! I could tell he almost giggled at my befuddlement, but he just smiled.

John was right. Seconds later I knew the answer. I wanted and needed to make a comeback. The dragons slain, the demons hushed, I could now play the football of my childhood dreams, without steroids and drugs. And I needed to do that *for me*. Some dreams just have to be fulfilled. I knew I had to finally try to make that one come true.

John Whyte sensed I'd finished my mission. He asked, "Are you finished? Did you ask him everything you needed to ask?"

"I'm done," I replied with a satisfied sigh. And then, before I turned to walk back up the two-track, a raven flew and landed on my brother John's right shoulder. It sat there as if on a very familiar perch—a midnight, jet-blue-black raven. I can still see it.

My brother spoke, "I am your spiritual guide. Even though you won't be able to see me as I am now in the world you live in, every time you see a raven, it's me there with you."

I nodded, astonished again, and this time comforted to know my brother would always be with me, even though I couldn't see him.

I turned and headed back up the two-track. John Whyte told me he would bring me back to Traverse City. A quarter of the way up the path, I turned back to look at my brother, expecting he had already disappeared. Wrong. He was still sitting there on the beach. I checked again half way up and he was still there. At the top of the two-track, I looked down once more, and John was still sitting by the fire with the bear hide around him.

I left the earth then, gaining altitude slowly over the Pacific Ocean. I kept looking back, seeing John's figure getting smaller and smaller as I drifted southeast over the Canadian forests. John Whyte brought me back over the Great Lakes and streams of Northern Michigan, and finally to the rooftop of my home. He brought me back through the roof, and back into my bed and into my body. He instructed me to stretch my fingers and hands and allow life to reenter my body. I was still unaware of time, but I think I lay there for several more minutes.

John Whyte and I talked about my journey. He didn't know my brother was my guide. He asked me what happened when I began crying. I told him I'd seen my brother.

"Did you get your answers, Tony?" He wanted to be sure my mission was complete.

"Yeah," I replied. "I made amends with John, and discovered he's my spiritual guide. I didn't get black and white answers about football, but now I know I have to go back and play. I have a dream that hasn't been fulfilled yet, and I have to try to make it happen without drugs and alcohol. I have to make the quiet amends with the game I love, the fans, my employers, all the people who believed in me and helped me. I have to try a comeback."

I began seeing ravens *daily!* My spiritual journey with John Whyte was one of the most profound experiences in my life. I questioned if I might have manifested it. And I still have to test John Whyte's extra-sensory perception gifts occasionally. In spite of my irritating need for confirmation, he never fails to reassure me.

Several times before I left Traverse City I called him. Before the telephone had a chance to ring, before the days of Caller ID, he answered and usually said, "Hi Tony. When are we going to work out?" His gifts are phenomenal and his friendship invaluable.

My spiritual journey was a huge turning point in my life. My willingness to relate to spiritual things opened the door for it to happen. I now notice ravens all the time; driving down a street, one will swoop in front of car; or walking into the office, a raven is perched in a tree nearby. It's been like that since my journey in 1995. My brother has been with me almost daily since then. He is still taking care of me.

Indianapolis Takes a Chance

"In one of those highly improbable but enlightening stories that transcends sports and hugs the human spirit, Mandarich has traveled full circle... (from) a disappointment to an inspiration."

Robin Miller, *Indianapolis Star*, December 13, 1996

Six months after treatment, I was feeling good. No, not good, *great!* I was back to 300 pounds and totally amazed that I was no longer a stick of a guy with my tail between my legs. I never thought I could do that without steroids. After I realized I could get and stay sober, I began to believe anything else I wanted to do was possible. Hope continued to grow in my life and I began to entertain the dreams spawned by that hope.

I attended AA meetings several times a week in Traverse City, but it took me six months to drum up the courage to actually talk in a meeting. I'd said I was new at the first few meetings I attended, but didn't share because I didn't feel I knew anything or had anything to share that would help anyone. I could relate to so many stories I heard; the details didn't matter. We all shared the tragedy of addiction. I knew AA was the right place for me when that commonality surfaced. Alcoholism doesn't discriminate. It's very patient.

Six months into sobriety, I finally talked about how I felt. The topic was gratitude and it was a regular meeting that I attended three times a week. I'd had a great day, and a great six months! I told myself that I needed to start sharing and being active in groups. I said,

"I feel great. I've had a fantastic day and six months. I haven't had a drink or drug. I thought the fun was over and laughter was gone when I stopped drugging and drinking. I thought the good times were gone, but I've found the complete opposite. Life has just begun. I've laughed more in these six months of sobriety than in the last 10 years. I'm carefree now, still unemployed, but employable! I'm okay financially, not great, not horrible. No money coming in, but still okay. It's going to work out. I'm staying sober and on track. I'm going to meetings, I don't drink; I pray a lot and meditate. It's so simple to do these things. Life is great and this program really does work!"

That's it. Just 30 seconds, but I finally shared in a meeting, and haven't stopped in the past 13 years. God had not condemned me to a life of addiction after all. I *chose* to drug and drink. It *was* possible for me to be sober, something I thought *impossible* just a few months previously. I now lived the miracle of sobriety every day. So if I wasn't doomed to be an alcoholic, and if I could live a sober life, just maybe I could also play football again—sober!

I began watching football again on weekends and told myself I could do better than some players I saw on national television. I thought, "If they can be in the starting line-up, I can do it too." My beliefs were changing. I was letting go of the notion that God intended me to be an alcoholic and to die an alcoholic death. I had believed that with every fiber of my body and soul, and spent years feeling morose and disappointed. In sobriety, however, I began to believe I could do anything I really wanted, and that 'anything' included football. I was recreating my goal of being a NFL player, but this time with a different direction and attitude.

That autumn, I became acutely aware of the wreckage I'd created and left behind. I knew the only way I could effectively make amends with my employers, fans and all those people I had wronged with arrogance and lack of productivity, was to try to play football again. This time I had to do it quietly, without all the hype and crass, loudmouth behavior. I had to give it 100% effort and make the quiet amends.

I took inventory again with my sponsor, writing my personal inventory that, this time, included all the wrongs I'd committed in the world of football. I shared that inventory with Amber and John Whyte, and they both supported my desire to make a comeback. Amber continued to be unbelievably supportive, in spite of the growing awareness that our marriage wasn't going to make it.

My foot speed had suffered the most. I'd been out of the League for three years. I knew I could get in shape again, but it would take time and commitment. I started playing racquetball five days a week, and continued to do that for the next six months; it offered the best practice for getting my foot speed back. I returned to the weight room five and six days a week. I practiced agility drills several days a week. I'd done all this before, when I did steroids and drugs, but this time was different. This time I was clean and dry and sober, and I was gaining strength, agility and stamina. I really missed football and now I just might have a chance to play again. My spirit soared!

I'd have to work out for NFL teams again to be considered, and I wanted to be sure I was ready for that. After six months of intense training by myself, I called my old friend and agent, Vern Sharbaugh, and told him I wanted to try out again for a team. I told him I was sober.

Vern was less than enthusiastic. The last time he saw me I was a drugged-up, burned-out disaster. He didn't want to put his reputation on the line again for a loser. I'm sure he pictured me flying in for a workout and embarrassing everyone, but he was also a friend and he was going to give me a chance.

"Come down here to Cleveland so I can see you," Vern instructed me, not sure he could believe I was sober.

Vern reacted visibly when he saw me. I was clear-eyed, and big and strong. He knew then I was for real.

He immediately put out some feelers and the Philadelphia Eagles responded. They weren't willing to fly me in to Philly for a workout, but a scout was flying through Cleveland with a six-hour layover.

Vern arranged for us to meet the scout at a community college, and the scout would work me out in the gym. I didn't blame them for their reluctance; nobody had heard from me for three years and they sure didn't want to waste money flying "The Incredible Bust" into Philadelphia for a workout.

We went to the community college gym and I went through the workout: agility drills specific to offensive linemen for about an hour, then into the weight room for bench press and squats. The workout with the Philly scout was very good, and he was impressed. Vern couldn't believe his eyes. The scout said they'd be in touch within 24 hours. The Eagles called Vern that night and told him they wanted to fly me out to Philadelphia and work me out for the head coach.

Then Vern made another call, this time to his friend, Ron Blackledge, offensive line coach with the Indianapolis Colts. Vern had been an assistant coach at Kent State when Ron Blackledge was head coach, so they knew each other well. Vern told Ron about my workout for the scout, and that Philly wanted to fly me out to work out for Ray Rhodes, their head coach. (Ray was an assistant coach when I was in Green Bay.) Ron responded by telling Vern the Colts would fly me to Indy for a workout within just a couple of days. A few days later I was on a plane to Indianapolis.

My head coach at Green Bay, Lindy Infante, was the offensive coordinator at Indianapolis at that time, and a month later was named head coach. I had known Ron Blackledge, the offensive line coach at Indy, since my brother John's Kent State days. In 1979, John and I drove to Kent State together; John was 18 and I was 13. Ron was head coach at Kent State University. He took John and me out to lunch at a little Italian joint in Kent. He talked with John about his chances for getting a scholarship and playing at Kent State. Ron told me that he wanted me to give him a call in a few years. He told me I was a big kid and I'd be playing football. He said he'd want me at Kent State. I was 13, 5'11", and 185 pounds. At age 13, I was totally impressed with Ron and that enhanced my desire to play football.

The next time I saw him, at age 29, was when I walked off the plane in Indianapolis in 1996. He waited for me at the gate. We greeted, and he chuckled, saying who would have thought in 1979 that we'd meet up again in Indy, him coaching here and me making a comeback.

Ron and one of their scouts, Clyde, worked me out. Lindy and Bill Tobin, the Colts General Manager, watched too. I had a good workout in the weight room and on the field. They were all impressed and saw my strength and agility. It was pretty incredible to all of us.

Lindy commented publicly about my comeback,

> "I'm telling you, he looked better on the hoof than when we looked at him in Green Bay. To us, it's a no-lose situation. If this works out and Tony shows he can play at this level, then it's a plus for us. That will make us a better football team. There is no question he has the tools. The challenge is for him to utilize them... In Green Bay... he was the phenom of all phenoms and the pressure on the guy was enormous. Here we just want him to come in and contribute."[13]

I did look better. Mike Chappell, sportswriter for The Indianapolis Star, referred to me as "...chiseled... at 325 pounds."[14] I was sober and clear-eyed, big and stronger than I'd ever been. (I squatted 680 that spring.) That was the first time Lindy ever saw me play drug-free. I hadn't had a sober day in Green Bay, including draft day and the Combine in Indy. I was 'sober' at the Combine (because they tested for drugs), but the lingering effect of steroids surely influenced my performance.

They wanted to sign me immediately and offered me a contract, but I had to be honest first. I told the head trainer and head physician that I'd gone through treatment and recovery. They needed

---

[13] Chappell, Mike. *Indianapolis Star.* "Colts Willing to Take Chance on Mandarich." February 23, 1996.
[14] IBID.

to know because of medical and prescription issues. They both treated it like it was no big deal. Their response made it easier to tell Lindy about my addiction.

Lindy had to know because, as the head coach, if he didn't want to take a gamble with a player like me, he had the right to make that decision. He asked what I'd been doing the past three years. I felt compelled to tell him.

"My life's been in shambles. I've been addicted to alcohol and prescription painkillers. I went into treatment 11 months ago and have been attending AA meetings since. I cleaned up and started working out again, trying to get back in the League. You were gracious enough to give me an opportunity to do that!" It was all true.

Lindy responded, "I'm glad you got help and got your life back on track. Thanks for telling me!"

So when the offer came, I knew they were okay with my past. I'd hid nothing and felt affirmed for telling the truth.

Now I really needed time to think. Less than 11 months before, I was drinking and drugging myself into an early grave. Now the Colts wanted me to sign a contract to play for them. I needed time, because I didn't want to make a rash decision. I definitely wanted to play again. My biggest concern was going back into the arena where I did all my drugging. I had to have some reassurance that I could play without drugging.

I went back to Traverse City and talked with my AA companions, the guys who'd been in sobriety 30 and 40 years. I had so many questions… Could I go back to the game and not drink and drug again? Will this threaten my sobriety? I messed up so badly before, will I do that again? I remembered they told me at Brighton only one in forty will maintain sobriety.

I needed assurance for my inner self and I was adamant I wouldn't ever sign a football contract with *any* team if it meant I might go backwards again. I wouldn't get in front of *that* locomotive. I've been there before and it wasn't a place I ever wanted to be again.

My AA friends reassured me. They told me to get my priorities right, go to meetings, get a new sponsor in Indy, and I'd be fine. They said I had to surround myself with good people. They were right. That's what I'd been doing since I got sober; attending meetings every day (sometimes twice a day), playing racquetball five times a week to get some foot speed back, hitting the weight room six times a week—I had put in a lot of time and effort trying to regain my ability to be able to perform well in those workouts.

Although Philly was also interested in talking with me, I signed a two-year contract with the Colts, who made the announcement with a press conference that got national attention. It was the middle of winter, but in spite of that the media came from all over the country. They wanted to know what was going on… why I was returning to football after my miserable years and all the negative press in my Green Bay days. One sports writer contrasted my salary with what I'd been paid by the Packers.

"Do you feel embarrassed to be making $196,000, compared to the $1.1 million you got at Green Bay?" His question bordered on incredulous.

"Absolutely not!" What I didn't say was, "*If you only knew how close I'd been to dying and not even being here.*" Part of my motivation was financial, to be sure, but mostly I needed to slay the dragons and make quiet amends. This time I was motivated to do it the professional way and keep my mouth shut. I needed to remove the bitter taste from my mouth about Green Bay and football. I was determined to make amends with fans, owners, coaches and people who love football as much as I do.

"Why are you coming back now? You're putting yourself out there at more risk of being ridiculed or getting bad press." It was another reasonable question.

"I have nothing to lose. You've written everything you could possibly write, I have nowhere to go but up. If I fail, I'm supposed to fail. Everything is a positive for me now." Again, what I didn't say was, "*I survived steroid use, drug abuse, failure, not living up to expectations… and now I get to prove to myself and the world that I can play sober."*

The tone of that press conference was entirely different from Draft Day, 1989. Seven years earlier, I ranted about being the best offensive lineman ever, and about how history would revere me. By February 1996, I'd become much more realistic and humble, a 180 degree turn from Green Bay days. Being sober made a huge difference too. It probably surprised the hell out of the reporters, but that wasn't my motive. I knew the way I did it before didn't work. From January 1989 to March 22, 1995, every quote of mine was made in an inebriated condition. I was either up from speed or down from downers, all under the flag of pharmaceutical drug abuse. I didn't have a clear mind during that time, and my vision was always blurred. I operated out of fear—fear of failure, of not living up to hype, of not being accepted, of people not liking me… you name it. I believe we humans create what we think about, and that's exactly what I created on a national level.

Sobriety changed me and I finally began to evolve as a person. The Colts' coaching staff knew I'd changed. Lindy knew it on a personal level. There were two different versions of Tony, and they liked the new one. I didn't give the media the details, but the coaches and medical team knew everything. They knew I needed to make quiet amends. Quiet was the operative word. I had to slay the demons to silence them in my mind.

JoAnn Barnas, Knight-Ridder Newspapers, wrote a story that describes that press conference much better than I can recall it.

"Tony Mandarich Eyeing NFL Comeback." April 30, 1996.

INDIANAPOLIS. He couldn't remember the last time he did this. Three television cameras were in the back of the room. A nest of tape recorders was on the podium in front of him.

Tony Mandarich scanned the room. He had just come from lifting weights. A blue bandanna do-rag was wrapped around his head. He wore gray shorts and a gray T-shirt with the collar cut out. On the back of the shirt were the words: 'Faster than a Fugitive from Hell—non-negotiable.'

Mandarich looked up at the clock, then out the window at a field of dandelions at the Indianapolis Colts training facility, where he's in the second month of his NFL comeback. When he was at Michigan State, he loved doing this—talking to a roomful of reporters, trying to think of clever and outrageous things to say.

Thursday, his first words at his first press conference in more than three years sounded humble.

'How are you guys doing?' he asked.

Then Tony Mandarich smiled. And he smiled some more because he couldn't believe he was doing this. See, Mandarich couldn't stay away. He's breaking the promise he made to himself when he walked away from pro football in February 1993.

Mandarich said he would never come back. Ever. Not to play football. Not to talk in front of the media. He wanted to forget everything about his pro playing days and remember only his career at Michigan State, where he was a three-year starter and All-American at offensive tackle.

'Football was fun then,' he said.

It stopped being that way almost the instant he left East Lansing in 1989.

Once he reached the pros, Mandarich never became the player his massive body suggested and college career proclaimed. The Green Bay Packers thought they had gotten their next Hall of Famer when they made him the second pick in the NFL draft, signing him to a four-year deal worth $4.4 million—the biggest contract in NFL history for an offensive lineman at the time.

But Mandarich never did a thing. He never redefined the position as he said he would. He wasn't even the best player on the team. He had held out for 45 days and never earned a start in his rookie season.

He started every game he played in 1990 and '91, but he was far from dominating. That was the last year he played. By 1992, Mandarich was suffering from a variety of ailments—post-concussion syndrome, a thyroid condition and a bacterial infection he said he caught while drinking from a creek during a bear hunt in Alberta, which caused him to lose 40 pounds in six weeks.

Mandarich also was dogged by repeated accusations of steroid abuse. And the person who drove him to play the game was gone now, too.

John Mandarich, Tony's older brother, died of cancer in February 1993 at age 31. John was the person who had convinced his parents, Vic and Donna Mandarich, who settled in Oakville, Ontario, after fleeing Yugoslavia in 1957, to let him become Tony's legal guardian. That way, Tony could live in Ohio his senior year of high school and learn how to play football 'the right way,' former MSU Coach George Perles remembered.

The other crushing blow came a few months earlier, in September 1993, when Sports Illustrated put Mandarich on its cover for the second time in four years. In 1989, the magazine had touted him as 'The Incredible Bulk.' This time, it called him 'The Incredible Bust.'

By February 1993, his contract at Green Bay having expired, Mandarich was gone.

'From what I read, Tony had been in isolation since he left football,' said Bob Kula, who played offensive guard at MSU in 1986-89. 'The story that I heard was the story in Sports Illustrated, the one that sandbagged him, was the one that did it. He's been through a lot of adversity. I'm sure it was tough for him to deal with. Look at Brian Bosworth. The same identical story, almost.'

For the last three years, Mandarich has been in virtual seclusion, living in a log house on 160 acres just outside

Traverse City with his wife, Amber, and 5 year-old daughter, Holly.

Football was the furthest thing from his mind. He gave his phone number to almost no one. He rarely watched games on television. Mandarich was determined to build a new life, so he took classes at Northwestern Michigan College in Traverse City to fulfill requirements needed to get into a law enforcement academy. Someday he wants to be a conservation officer.

But on the way to class one day in September 1995, something happened.

'I did a lot of praying,' Mandarich said. 'I was walking to class and I asked myself, 'If there is anything you want to be doing right now, what would you be doing?' I wanted to play football. I had missed it. But what I had missed more than anything was having fun playing it because it had been such a long time, and you can hold on to the past and to those stories for so long.'

So now, at age 29, Mandarich is beginning a career he never really had. He's starting over, one last time, trying to fix the past because he doesn't like the way it ended the first time.

'It was a lesson in humility, and I took the good out of it,' Mandarich said. 'I'm trying to change it for Tony, not anybody else. You can change how you're remembered, but I can't change what happened in Green Bay.'

The time away also has made Mandarich realize something else: He missed football more than it missed him.

And Thursday, he was saying the words no one ever thought possible seven years ago—a far cry from his days at MSU. Then he said his goals included 'a national championship, being the first lineman drafted in the next NFL draft, winning the Super Bowl® and becoming Mr. Universe after my playing days.'

In a crowded press room in Indianapolis, Mandarich fumbled a bit as he summed up his comeback.

'I can't say my goal is to come back and make the Pro Bowl®,' he said. 'That's too far away.'

That wasn't what he wanted to say, either. He started again.

'The next goal for me is not to start, OK?' Mandarich said. 'It's to make the team. Thinking too far ahead got me off focus in Green Bay. I'll give my heart and soul—my all—to this team. I didn't want it to end the way it did. I didn't like the way it ended in Green Bay.

'I want to come back and have fun playing the game. I haven't had fun playing the game since I left college. That wasn't Green Bay's fault. That was my fault.'

Maybe pro football will be a part of his life again. Maybe it won't. Ask Colts Coach Lindy Infante about his newest free-agent signee, and he says bluntly, 'I don't think the expectations are exceptionally high. If Tony could make our roster, it would be a plus for us.'

Terms of his two-year deal weren't disclosed but Mandarich said he was making the 'bare minimum,' which would be $196,000 if he made the opening day roster.

Currently he's drawing the same salary as all of the veterans who begin mini-camp workouts on Friday: $750 a week.

Mandarich said he was tested for drugs before he reported to camp, which 'was fine with me.' He will be tried out at tackle or guard—'too tall to be a center,' said Mandarich, 6'5"—but he does not care where he ends up. He just wants to play.

A year ago, before he started working out again, Mandarich weighed 265 pounds. He's now up to almost 325—thanks to the weight room, he said. This week, Mandarich bench-pressed 435 pounds and squatted 680—'most on the team,' he said, smiling.

Entering the 1989 draft, Mandarich could squat-lift 550 and was timed in 4.65 seconds for the 40-yard dash. In the 21 years the National Scouting Combine had been rating draft-eligible college players, only Bo Jackson and Herschel Walker had graded higher than Mandarich's overall 8.5 on a scale of 10. They had 9.0s.

'Benching 545 coming out of college didn't help me pass-block,' Mandarich said. 'That's the way I look at it. I just want to help this team. This (tryout) will answer a whole ton of questions for me.'

It will, too, for Infante. This will be his second time around with Mandarich.

Infante, hired in mid-February to replace Ted Marchibroda, coached the Packers in 1988-91 and was instrumental in signing Mandarich.

'When we drafted him in 1989, we had the second pick and by league standards we believed what everybody believed,' Infante said. 'I'm sure there's some people who would say they didn't feel that way at the time, but I'm not sure they're being totally honest. He was projected as a can't-miss Pro Bowl®-type player, a player who would be around for 12 years and solidify an offensive line spot for a long time.

'It didn't turn out that way. I think there was a great deal of hype that was created by Tony and his agent, in particular. The longer he was out (during his holdout), the bigger the stories got about how much he can dominate. But nobody in our league does that. There was some kind of myth created that he was doing to destroy people in the National Football League, and nobody does that.'

Mandarich's life today is many years removed from the sitcom it once was. He used to promote himself incessantly and appeared on the David Letterman and Pat Sajak talk shows. He even appeared on an episode of the comedy series 'Dear John.' And remember the hoopla that Mandarich might fight Mike Tyson for $10 million?

About the only permanent reminders he has from those days are on his biceps and ankles—tattoos of an Alaskan brown bear, two designs celebrating the rock band Guns 'n' Roses, the Harley-Davidson logo and two strands of barbed wire.

But mention the Tyson hype, and Mandarich starts laughing.

'Hey, not everything I did was bad,' he said. 'I think I brought some positives into the league. I feel I made offensive linemen a lot more money—I'm talking pre-salary cap days.

'You know what makes it easier? If it doesn't work out here, I know I didn't hold anything back. I did everything I had to do to prepare for this. If I don't make it, hey, that episode of this journey's done.

'Football is just a small part of my life. It's not what I am. It's something I do."[15]

Another sports writer from the Detroit News captured part of what I felt during that press conference; "He is on a mission from nowhere, seeking something that can be defined only in his soul…"[16] My soul and my heart knew how deeply I wanted to play football, and do it right this time. He saw someone who grew up a little bit, and didn't do it for anybody but himself. I needed to change the ending and have some redemption, make amends without calling it that at the time. He saw what I was feeling. I didn't have to explain it to him. He just saw it. I was in the 'do it for me'-place. All I had to do was try again, sober this time.

The quote by Robin Miller at the beginning of this chapter is significant in part because he wasn't a favorite beat writer for the

---

[15] Barnas, JoAnn. *Detroit Free Press.* "Tony Mandarich Eyeing NFL Comeback." April 4, 1996.

[16] O'Hara, Mike. *The Detroit News.* "Mandarich Tries Comeback, Looking for a Better Endng." April 26, 1996.

Colts. He was always rather critical. Every team has a sportswriter like that. So the positive flavor of his comment about my comeback means just that much more to me, as he could have remained critical, but didn't.

I eagerly anticipated the chance to compete and do what I originally wanted to do: play football well. I was one of the strongest guys on the team, and I had gotten there without steroids. *Why in the world did I think I needed them in the first place?* Joel Buchsbaum's Scout's Notebook column in Pro Football Weekly from July 1996, said of my arrival in Indianapolis, "[Tony] is bigger and stronger than he has been at any time since he left college... An intriguing long shot who could go from being one of the greatest draft busts ever to one of the league's more amazing comeback stories."[17]

Although the workout was pretty incredible, given the past three years, I wasn't assured of a contract until after summer camp in Anderson, Indiana. There were 80 guys there, and only 53 of us would make the cut. Making this hurdle was a big deal for me. For the first time in four years, I donned shoulder pads and began hitting guys on the field, moving them around. I began to realize I could still play football. Some guys were cut during the six weeks of camp. I had a good feeling as those weeks passed, believing I would make the 53-man roster. The coaches were giving me a lot of playing time and my practices went well. The films looked good. Coaches were talking with me about the upcoming season.

By the last week of camp, I had a pretty good idea I'd make it; I knew who was playing well and who wasn't. I probably wouldn't be in the starting lineup, but I was playing well enough to make the team. The day arrived when the final cuts list was posted... and my name wasn't on it. I whispered a prayer of gratitude to God for my family, my sobriety and the Indianapolis Colts. I knew my sobriety was the thread that gave me the opportunity to come back. There wasn't any defining moment, just the gradual development of

---

[17] Buchsbaum, Joel. *Pro Football Weekly.* Scout's Notebook. July, 1996.

knowledge and strength that allowed me the opportunity to try to play football once again.

My teammates and coaches congratulated me with genuine hearts and sincerity. They'd been pulling for me and were happy I made the roster. That was a huge time of redemption for me. After all the negativity that characterized my relationships with other players in Green Bay, I felt accepted by my fellow Colts as a member of the team for the first time in my NFL career.

11

A New Experience: Playing Sober

My Roman Catholic upbringing taught me God has a plan for every person's life. I even believed the Bible reference about counting the hairs on my head, just because He cared about me (and because that's what the Bible says, given a literal translation). As my drug and alcohol abuse increased, and my life deteriorated, I understood unquestioningly God's plan for me was to be a miserable alcoholic and die an alcoholic death.

I remember well the day that belief cracked and broke into a thousand little pieces. Oh my God! He didn't intend for me to be an alcoholic! I made the choice to abuse drugs and alcohol. It wasn't God doing that to me. It was me doing that to myself! That happened in treatment at Brighton. Then, after the Indianapolis Colts signed me to a two-year contract and I completed training and made the team, I had another Oh my God! experience. I realized I was given the opportunity to play football again. God gave me a do-over and the Colts opened the door for it to happen. How miraculous!

One of the pieces of the sobriety puzzle that really worked for me was praying and asking for help every day. I still pray daily. I thank God for sobriety and ask for guidance, patience, humility and courage, and that I give everything I can give in every activity that day and hold nothing back.

I find myself praying throughout the day now. It's just God and me, and we talk a lot.

I still consider myself Catholic; I would go to a Catholic church if I had to choose, but my vision of God has expanded. My God is not a punishing God any longer. All the lies, cheating, stealing and conning deserve punishment in my old belief system. I got sober and now I have a great life. That threw a monkey wrench into the Catholic belief system of a punishing God. Now I have a loving and forgiving higher power. I'm glad I didn't get what I believed I deserved.

My comeback game was both exhilarating and nostalgic. We played in the Hall of Fame game, a kickoff to preseason. It's always played in Canton, Ohio, where the Football Hall of Fame is located. My brother John and I went to Canton to visit the Hall of Fame when we lived in Kent, and those memories flooded my senses when I returned to play my first game after three years in hiding.

We played the New Orleans Saints. Willie Roaf, all pro offensive tackle for the Saints, came up to me after the game and said, "It's really good to see you back!"

I hadn't known Willie before that, and I had never spoken to him. But, *WOW!* It really felt good to hear him say that. My previous NFL experience was the opposite. The players on the NFL teams considered me a bigmouth asshole. And I was. This was a whole new experience for me and I knew I was finally doing something right.

Holding nothing back, I gave Indy everything I had. Even after the 11 months of preparation and training, I worked hard in the weight room, kept running and doing agility drills in off-season to stay in shape, and took good care of my body. I was determined to make amends with my game and my friends. I knew if I didn't make it, at least I gave myself the best possible opportunity. I was finally able to put on my shoulder pads and helmet and start playing football again. It was incredibly satisfying and redemptive.

The season opener, always awesome in the NFL, was with the Arizona Cardinals at Indianapolis. The entire country was excited about football again. By this time, we knew who made the team and who didn't. When the national anthem started, I realized how grateful I was to have a second chance. I was 18 months sober and playing in the NFL again. No longer a zombie doing drugs 24/7, I was living my original dream of playing in the NFL. Goosebumps covered my body, both because of the national anthem and because I was standing on the sideline, hand over my heart and grateful to be alive. God does allow do-overs.

I made my first start since Green Bay when we played Washington in October 1996. Mike Chappell, staff writer for the Indianapolis News, wrote,

> "He more than held his own and had been due to assume another heavy workload the following week against San Diego. But Mandarich injured his shoulder early in the game, missing the second half and the following game at Miami... Quarterback Jim Harbaugh hopes the changes at tackle will result in better protection than he was provided when the Colts first met the Patriots. In a 27-9 loss last month, Harbaugh was sacked three times and knocked from the game in the fourth quarter with a broken nose."[18]

The shoulder injury plagued me from that moment on, but I was finally back where I wanted to be. I was in the starting lineup of my team, playing well and having fun. Six months after I signed with Indianapolis, Tom Zupancic, the strength coach for the Colts, said to me, "You know, it's gotta feel pretty damn good to have walked into this weight room six months ago and now know that you've taken it over! Nobody's stronger than you. You were out of football all those years, and now you're back and you're the strongest! That's gotta feel pretty damn good!" Tom played a major role in all that. He was instrumental in my comeback.

When we traveled to play AFC East rival, the New England Patriots, Ron Blackledge told me I'd be starting for the second time at right tackle. Jason Matthews had played that position for all 26 of his NFL starts; he was being moved to left tackle. When the press asked Ron about the shift, he said, "I don't know how much Tony is going to play, but I really want to see him out there. He has done

---

[18] Chappell, Mike. *The Indianapolis News*. "Mathews Will Tackle Left Side to Make Room for Mandarich." November 23, 1996.

some pretty good things for us."[19] I was in the starting lineup from that point on. I was playing football again; that's why I was there.

In December, after the changes in our offensive line, a story in the Indianapolis Star made reference to my comeback. "The emergence of Mandarich, arguably the National Football League's comeback player of the year, permitted the Colts to move Mathews to the left side."[20] Jim Harbaugh "... praised a revamped offensive line for the change in his environment."[21] Four weeks earlier Jim had been sacked unmercifully. We were there to do our job, to protect Jim. I did a good job playing at Indy. I was proud to be part of the new offensive line that changed our game plan that year and put us in the playoffs.

My nature is aggressive, which created the greatest challenge for me with the Colts. My size probably contributes more than a little to the level of aggression that I'm comfortable with. Ron Blackledge mentioned this in an article Mike Chappell wrote in the summer of 1996. (Mike referred to me as a 'behemoth tackle' in this article.)

> "Aggressiveness may be an attribute in fire-out run blocking, but unchecked aggression can be a detriment in pass protection where a fall-back-and-react philosophy prevails.
>
> 'Tony is so full of enthusiasm' said Blackledge. 'He wants to do the job, but sometimes he's over-aggressive.'"[22]

I was taught from high school to make mistakes at full speed; I'd get hurt if I played at half speed. I also had to prove to other players that I wasn't going to back down from anybody. So I was probably more aggressive than I'd been previously. Just because my perspective about life and living changed, I wasn't going to be a doormat. I was more level headed than ever before in my adult life,

---

[19] IBID.

[20] Bansch, John. *Indianapolis Star*. "Colts Put Credit on Offensive Line." December 18, 1996.

[21] IBID.

[22] Chappell, Mike. *Indianapolis Star*. "Mandarich Makes Headway in his Comeback. August 2, 1996.

but I kept my level of aggression on the field at the absolute top of the scale.

Aggression in run blocking is okay; but aggression in pass blocking isn't. I needed to learn to be more balanced and have more patience than ever before. I wouldn't make mistakes because of speed or lack of effort, but I did learn how to be more balanced and more patient. My first season with the Colts was the first time since my senior year of high school that I played sober, drug-free and alcohol-free. That was 13 years ago, in 1983. This was a whole new experience for me and I definitely had a lot to learn.

We traveled to Pittsburgh for the playoffs and lost, but we'd played well and I felt good. There I was, 30 years old, in the playoffs of the National Football League. The whole experience felt surreal to me again. The contrast between that year and the previous year astounded me. Sitting in my apartment in Indy, I remembered how I couldn't get off the couch just 12 months ago. My thoughts had been consumed with drinking and drugging, isolating myself, and trying to figure out how to get and do drugs. Then in 12 miraculous and incredible months, I was employable again, a productive member of society. A lot of work went into my comeback, but I knew in advance what it would take to get there; I'd been there once before. And then, there I was, in the playoffs.

Although Jerome Bettis, the running back for Pittsburgh, received the NFL Comeback Player of the Year Award for 1996, I was humbled when the Colts organization bestowed the team honor on me. The Colts Comeback Player Award was split between Richard Dent and myself that year. He led the team in sacks. They gave me the chance to return to football, and it meant more to me than the NFL honor would have.

Not only did I play football as I'd originally dreamed, my attitude about playing was drastically different from my Green Bay days. Don Pierson, a writer for the Chicago Tribune, interviewed me and said this,

"Talk about a kid with a new toy. Tony Mandarich is a man who turned a nightmare into a dream. It is a surprise Christmas gift to himself that is still being unwrapped.

"A year after glancing at the Colts in the playoffs on a TV monitor at the racquetball courts in Traverse City, Michigan, Mandarich starts at right tackles for the Colts against the Steelers Sunday in Pittsburgh.

"Four years out of football, the man drafted behind Troy Aikman and ahead of Barry Sanders in 1989 is the comeback story of the year on the comeback team of the NFL.

"'Tony has been a real—I don't want to say surprise— but maybe that's a good word,' Colts coach Lindy Infante said.

"It's the only word."[23]

The Colts were the 'comeback' team of the NFL that year, due in part to the offensive line change. We started out 4-0, dropped to 6-6, and then came back to the playoffs and another run at the Super Bowl®. I'd first started because of injury on the offensive line, but soon was starting "… because he has earned the job."[24]

I'm the first to admit starting was just a detail. The real job for me, the real *daily* task, was to stay on target with my sobriety and keeping my attitude clean. I no longer needed to be the 'best' lineman in the world. I reminded myself daily that I always needed to look for where I could improve, where I needed to change.

We were playing the Eagles in Indianapolis, and kicking their butts. It was 31-0 with ten minutes left in the game. It was hot and I was sweating like crazy; my leg muscles cramp badly if I get dehydrated. We made another touchdown, and went up 38-0. The game was almost over, and the second guy in my position went in to replace me. Then my quads started cramping up. The trainer saw the

---

[23] Pierson, Don. *Chicago Tribune.* "An Attitude Adjustment in Indy." December 26, 1996.

[24] IBID.

anguish on my face and they took me off the field to the locker room, telling me they were going to start an IV. As we walked off the field, both my hamstrings started cramping along with my quads. I couldn't stretch either way to alleviate the pain because both sets of muscles were on fire. When we arrived in the locker room, I said to the trainer and assistant,

"I'm two years sober. Both my legs are locked up but I can't do Valium."

My muscles were as hard as the table I lay on. The physician had the IV ready, wanting to inject the meds that would release the cramps. I just couldn't allow that. I went through 30 more minutes of excruciating pain. I think it's the worst physical pain I've ever experienced, even worse than the withdrawal had been. After the cramps finally released their stranglehold on my legs, we troubleshot the cause. It was humid; I drank too much coffee and I was dehydrated. I thought we'd all learned something from figuring it out.

We made the playoffs and went to Pittsburgh to play against the Steelers. It was December 28 and unseasonably warm at 60 degrees. At half time, my quads began their rampage again. We were in the locker room at half time, and my legs cramped. Blood was pooling in my legs and they were locking up again. This episode was less than a month after the previous one. The team doc had the IV ready and looked at me with raised eyebrows. He knew how much pain I endured just a month earlier.

"OK. I give up. I'm not going through that again. Give me the Valium." The emotional turmoil was almost as bad as the physical pain. Here I was agreeing to pain-killing medications in my body again, the same kind of drugs that wrecked my life for seven years.

As the doc was setting up the IV equipment, I lay on the table praying it wouldn't send me off on a huge relapse; I was terrified of that possibility. When the drug hit my system, the relief was instant. I felt the cramps let go. I couldn't believe how quickly they disappeared. I didn't get high at all. I now realize my motivation was not to get high; it was to get relief from my leg cramps.

After the game, we flew back to Indy. We arrived by six o'clock and I immediately picked up my sponsor and we went to a meeting. I talked about it with him and at the meeting. I didn't want to keep it a secret and I needed their help. I told them I hadn't felt high at all, but the pain relief was almost immediate. They all reassured me that it comes down to motive. If my motive was to get medical relief, I needed to know that was different from getting high. I felt a lot of support for my choice and my motivation. But it was a huge scare because painkillers were my drugs of choice, and I knew my life was over if I relapsed.

Now I'm extremely leery about what I put into my system. Over-the-counter Advil is all I'll take. When I had to have shoulder surgery, I was anesthetized. Following surgery, I was given a script for 20 Vicodin. I never filled it and instead took 1600mg of Advil for pain and inflammation. It's amazing to me how strong your body and mind are when you want them to be. The contrasts are incredible… shooting up in the locker room, and then refusing to take drugs, then admitting I needed drugs administered by a physician for pain relief. Where my mind was at the time made all the difference in the world.

Jim Harbaugh, the quarterback for the University of Michigan when I was at MSU, is both a great guy and a great football player. He is very down to earth; I've always admired him. Jim was always positive and encouraging with me, never belittling or demeaning me because of my past history. He is a very decent man. He and Tom Zupancic made a big impact on my life in Indy. Tom, my strength coach, pushed me to places I didn't think I could get to in my workouts. He's one of the few people in the world that I've encountered who could push harder than I could. We're still good friends.

Not all players greeted my comeback warmly. In San Diego, we were facing the Chargers and defensive back, Rodney Harrison, a big mouth that liked to jaw a lot during games. The first year we played against them, he taunted me on the field, saying I should get off steroids. I jawed back. I don't remember what I said, but I remember his reference to steroids. When I thought about it later, it didn't bother me so much because I knew what my life had really been like, and I knew this time in the NFL I wasn't on steroids. I was big and strong again and I'd done it without chemical assistance. I didn't have to defend myself to him. He was just another player. I probably responded with a comment about his mother or his wife. Sometimes taunts on the field would get to that level if you got pissed off enough. I wasn't going to be anybody's doormat just because I was sober, but I also wasn't going to be a loudmouth. I found it ironic that in 2007, Rodney Harrison served a four game suspension for violating the NFL substance abuse policy by using human growth hormones. Way to go, Rodney!

I recall an incident when we played the Kansas City Chiefs; my teammates and I were warming up in the end zone. Seats at the Chiefs' stadium come right up to the end zone. Their fans, only a few feet away, screamed at me, "You suck! You're a loser! You shouldn't even be in the NFL!"

I chuckled inside; it was amazing to me that I was even there. I could easily have been dead. I was just grateful to be there, listening to their insults. They paid for their tickets and they were entitled to say what they wanted to say. I was happy to be alive!

I felt accepted by my teammates. There was no taunting from them about my past failures. We all worked hard. I was really happy to hear from Bill Tobin toward the end of my first year—he told me my second year salary would jump from $196,000 to $500,000, and in my third year with the Colts I reached the $1 million mark again.

However, money was no longer the sole motivation for me, like it had been in Green Bay. I resolved that it would not be a problem for me with the Colts. I had allowed money and media to affect me too much before, both positively and negatively. I answered a lot of questions for myself and made some good progress working on my life-lessons, and I didn't let the media and money get in the way this time. Before my comeback, I thought all I had to do was work harder than anybody else and get the edge on the game. By the time I began playing regularly for Indy, I also realized I had to do the *right* things.

Even when my third year with the Colts rolled around, I never chose to get complacent. I chose to continue to want to play football and have fun. Mike Chappell interviewed me several times over the years, always writing without bias and without vendetta.

Referring to my Green Bay Packer years, he wrote, "He was larger than life and easy to dislike. Now a Colt, he's approachable, personable and grateful he was given the chance to atone for mishandling those days in Green Bay."[25] I felt comforted to know the media wrote *nice* things about me. My efforts to maintain my attitude change paid off.

We played Green Bay on Sunday, November 16, 1997. The Packers were the defending Super Bowl® Champions that year and I was ready for the game. I started at right tackle. That meant Reggie White stood opposite me on the line.

Reggie White, the Packers defensive end, had a team-high record 6.5 quarterback sacks, which increased his NFL-record total to 172 that year. He'd been playing for 13 years and at 35, was probably looking at retiring. Although he was past his prime, he was still a very good player, much better than average. I always admired and respected Reggie because he's such a good football player, in spite of his scolding me about my profanity on the field several years earlier.

Notwithstanding a sprained ankle I'd suffered the previous week, I didn't give up any sacks to Reggie that day, or to any of the Packers, and he didn't toss me around the field like he'd done when he was with Philly and I was with Green Bay. Two things were different that day. We had both changed teams, and I made sure he never got close to our quarterback. We beat the defending champions that day, 41-38. They were 10-0 for the season, and we beat them. I had fun staring at, and sparring with, Reggie that day.

---

[25] Chappell, Mike. *Indianapolis Star.* "Colts' Mandarich Not Getting Too Comfortable." August, 1997.

At the end of the 1997 season, Lindy Infante told Mike O'Hara of The Detroit News,

> "Tony's had a real solid season. He worked his way back into playing shape. He's gotten steadily better. He's been a real bright spot for us. I think he's played real solid football. It's really kind of a success story for a young man who has been abused by the media for not living up to his expectations in Green Bay."[26]

Lindy saw my work first hand because he was the Packers' head coach in Green Bay. He was present for both of my football experiences, so he had a perspective not available to any others. Thanks for the kind words, Lindy.

In March 1998, just before the Combine, I was offered a $3 million, three-year contract with the Chicago Bears. I signed the offer sheet and told Bill Tobin. Indy's contract with me included a third year option, with Indy holding a right to first refusal. We'd tried to negotiate with them, but Indy wasn't offering me anything above base salary. So I went shopping and the Bears made me an offer.

They'd flown me to Chicago, and after an initial interview, had me work out. I also underwent a physical with their medical team. We talked briefly about terms of a contract, and their offer was on the table: three years, $3 million. I knew I could be moving within a few weeks if the Colts didn't want to match the offer.

But within hours, the Colts made me the same offer and I signed for another three years with Indy. I'm glad they matched it, because Indy gave me the chance to return to football and I really wanted to stay. Club President Bill Polian said it was important to retain a veteran lineman like me, particularly because of the anticipated makeup of the team's offensive line in 1998.

At that time, I'd started 53 games during the six years I'd played, all at right tackle. The previous year, I started all 16 games, again all at right tackle. But it was a poor year for the Colts, and Lindy

---

[26] O'Hara, Mike. *The Detroit News.* "Mandarich Learned His Lesson." November 20, 1997.

Infante was fired and replaced by Jim Mora. I didn't know what he thought of me, but I soon learned. He moved me from tackle to right guard. I was happy with the move. Jim said,

> "Mandarich is proving to be a big contributor to what we believe will be a better offense. I'm certainly glad we decided to match his offer and keep him. He's been one of our best workers thus far."[27]

I wasn't going to fail because of a lack of effort. Talent, maybe, but not effort. That's why we were here... to do our job. I think I was better situated at guard than tackle. Howard Mudd came to the organization about the same time Jim Mora arrived. Howard was a great offensive line coach; he's still with the Colts.

I never lost track of what kept me going, what kept me sober and playing again; God and my commitment to following the Alcoholics Anonymous plan.

I attended both AA and NA meetings in Traverse City and Indianapolis. My key problem was drugs, and I discovered a younger crowd in NA. So most of my meetings in Traverse City were NA meetings. When I moved to Indy, I experienced the NA group living in the problem more than the solution, and that didn't work as well for me. I'm not knocking NA; it works for millions of people. I just found that AA worked better for me; I found more growth in AA than I did in NA in Indy, so that's where I spent most of my time in meetings. I believe every addict has to find the combination of meetings that work for him or her.

I finally debuted as a speaker in Indianapolis at an AA meeting. I was just under two years sober. It was a small Friday night meeting, one I attended regularly. There were only 20 people there. The secretary asked me three weeks prior if I would speak. I agreed, feeling a little anxious. I wasn't crazy about public speaking, and especially talking about my personal life in public, but it turned out

---

[27] Lowenkron, Hank. *Johnson County Daily Journal.* "Mandarich Big Part of Rejuvenated Line." June 12, 1998.

to be a great experience. I told my story, with no lies and no half-truths—just the gruesome journey.

Since then I've spoken in AA meetings over 100 times in the past 13 years. The story changes as my life evolves. Life goes on and my experiences get added as I speak. I have a new experience in sobriety every day, and my story also changes as I work the steps. Recovery changes for all of us with the passing years.

I'm treated like everyone else at AA meetings; I'm just another drunk there. We're at meetings for a reason, and that is to stay sober, get help, and help others. We never have problems with people who are there for that reason. Once in a while, someone asks me for an autograph in a meeting.

I always say, *"No, not here. See me in the parking lot after the meeting."* That's not a place to ask for an autograph. I'm there for sobriety, not to sign autographs. I told my sponsor about that once and he laughed.

"They're ignorant!" he said.

When the time finally came, some of my AA friends didn't want me to go to Canada. They tried to get me to stay in Indy, but it was time for me to go home. I had a lot of closure on a lot of grief with my success in Indianapolis and with the Colts. Those years allowed me to look at the big picture. This wasn't about football. It was about my journey into AA and sobriety.

The Foxhole Prayer

"Bidden or not bidden, God is present"

Reply from Delphic Oracle to the Spartans
when they planned war against Athens.

Roman Catholic beliefs governed lives in my family. My mother is the epitome of a devout Catholic woman. My dad is very committed to his religion and even more to his faith, but somehow 'devout' just doesn't describe my dad. Even though divorced and remarried, he still considers himself a Catholic. Because of their difficult life in Croatia, the Catholic Church became the center of their lives. Since they were very hands-on parents, it was also the center of John's and my life.

I was baptized and confirmed in the Church. I did the altar boy thing, too. We lived in Oakville, Ontario, where a large settlement of Croatians had migrated. The community was large enough to support Holy Trinity Croatian Catholic Church.

I had a love-hate relationship with the Church as a child. We participated in everything related to the Church and attended services faithfully every Sunday. I didn't like going and I didn't like having to participate in all the activities. It could have been a Buddhist Temple, Lutheran church, or whatever; I just didn't like going because I didn't like being told what to do. I wanted to stay home, but I went because my parents made me go. They felt they had an obligation as parents to raise us in the Church.

In retrospect, I'm glad they did, and I'm glad I went to church. I got to experience all those things and I get to compare them now. I know what I prefer and what I don't. I didn't have bad experiences with religion; those experiences helped me form opinions about what

I believe today, and the thread of religion has always been compelling in my life.

God was punitive and demanding when I was a child and before I became sober. I feared God, especially when I did something the church said was wrong. I believed God had a 'plan' for everyone, including me. And until sobriety, I believed God put me on this earth to be a drug addict; I had no choice in the matter. I was supposed to drink and do drugs, and die an alcoholic death somewhere in a gutter.

That fatalistic belief came from all the dos and don'ts I learned in church. It felt to me like the church had an opinion on just about everything in its attempts to control people. I believed that if I didn't follow every prescription handed down by the church, I was going to burn in hell.

Then, as an adult, I found myself drinking and drugging to an early grave. I still believed in God and had faith every day. I never blamed God. I accepted the belief that God put me on earth to do something, and I got the short end of the stick because I became a drug addict. That's the role I was meant to play in society. The only reason God brought me to this earth for this lifetime was to be an active alcoholic and active drug addict. I thought you had to play the cards that you were dealt.

I would much rather have been a doctor or a lawyer or somebody in high society with a nice life, but I had accepted the addict role. I believed that was God's plan for my life. I lived it. I'd sometimes sit there and think, "*Man, what would it be like if I didn't have to drink and drug every day?*" I'd sometimes go four or five days without drinking and then compulsions, mental obsessions and physical need would take over. It was His plan. The compulsions became God talking to me. I thought even if it was possible to be physically sober from drugs and alcohol, all the fun would be gone. The fun was in the bottle and the syringe.

When the miracle of sobriety happened for me, everything changed. A month without a drink or drug hadn't happened since high school, if you include steroids. Miraculously, then, I was sober and I was happy! Sixty days into sobriety, I had found myself laughing my butt off and enjoying life, and actually finding peace and serenity and comfort in my own skin without having to be chemically assisted. For me that was earth shattering.

My whole world changed—both my outlook and attitude on life. The magical Paradigm Shift occurred and my outlook on life transformed. My shift went from, "*What's in it for me?*" to "*How can I help?*" It's a huge perception change for living one's life. I now think about how I can help someone else, how I can be of service in my small corner of the world.

Gratitude is a good practice; it makes you reflect. It's so much about perception. I try to be grateful every day, even though I don't always measure up to that standard. On the days when I'm not very grateful, I'm still thanking God for my sobriety and if that's my worst kind of day, then that's okay.

When new opportunities arrive now, I look to see what I can pack into the stream of life rather than suck from it. God was always there, I just had my back turned. There weren't any fireworks or drum roll; now I just look at life differently.

Laughing is my elixir for most of life now. It's important to be able to laugh at yourself and not take yourself too seriously. I spent too many years wasting time so now that I've gotten sober, I find myself laughing a lot. I want to spend my time experiencing things that I want to experience, those that create joy for me. Now my fireworks come from laughter. God has a sense of humor and I can laugh now, too. I realized all this during that gut-busting laughter episode at Brighton Hospital in Michigan.

That night my religious belief system also began to change. I wondered if I was not supposed to die a gutter drunk; maybe I was not supposed to be a drunk at all. The God of my understanding changed. I realized it was no longer God's plan for me to be addicted, and probably never had been. I did all that to myself. My fatalistic attitude of, "If you do harm to others and harm to yourself, God will punish you," was eroding.

Here I was, a guy that had done a lot of harm to family, self, and others. How come I was blessed with the miracle of sobriety? I began to see the opportunity to help other alcoholics recover, which in turn helps me in my recovery. What is my role here? Couple all those changes, from living with a punishing God all my life, to suddenly getting another chance – it's unbelievable. How can a jackass like me get this miracle? It doesn't make sense to me. I've done too much harm, created too much ill will. I should be dead or in hell. How come now the miracle has happened? Why this gift? A lot of my beliefs changed at that time.

I still don't have the answers to all those questions, but I know I have a different relationship with God now. In sobriety, my beliefs are different and now I find God forgiving and loving.

The next shift occurred when I realized I could and would play football again. If I did it right and made amends, the circle would come fully around and I'd live my childhood dreams of playing in the NFL. The circle came round, and my dreams were fulfilled. So it's not surprising that God played a role in my decision to retire from professional football.

My shoulder sustained numerous assaults over the years, and it was beginning to bother me a lot. During one of the games in Indianapolis, I wrenched it severely and was unable to finish the game. Even though I'd had treatment for the pain, I always went back into the fire before it was completely healed. With my years of weightlifting, practice and games, I got to the point where I couldn't raise my arm over my head.

Two things happened that led me to make the decision to retire. Toward the end of the fourth quarter of the last game I played, against the Miami Dolphins, I cracked a bone in my back. There wasn't much time left, and I didn't play the rest of the game. Back in Indianapolis, following diagnostic tests, the cracked bone was identified, and my back and upper torso were immobilized in a brace for five weeks. It kept me from twisting my back and re-injuring the bone. There were six games left in the year. It was a five-week injury, so the Colts put me on injured reserve for the balance of the year.

That meant I couldn't come back to play even if I recovered quickly. The crack did heal, but I didn't play anymore.

The second incident involved my chronically injured shoulder. I never let up with my weightlifting, so my shoulder bothered me continually. Even after surgery, it never fully recovered. My choices were to keep battering it and watch it get worse and face replacement surgery at some point, or use painkillers for the rest of the year.

I wouldn't even consider painkillers. That was a no-brainer.

After the game where I really hurt it badly again, I suddenly remembered the Foxhole Prayer I had with God before I signed with the Colts. When I got sober and started putting weight back on, I began wondering how I could make amends for the mess I made with my employment and for how I embarrassed football. I thought if I comeback and make it and keep my mouth shut and do the right thing, it would be a silent amend. So I said to God, "I'll make a deal. If you let me go back and let me play, I'll do this right. I'll make amends and slay my dragons and quiet my demons. And then I'll walk away from the game when those things are accomplished."

Well, I had slain my dragons and exorcised my demons; I accomplished what I wanted. I played sober for the first time in my professional life and I played pretty well. I kept my mouth shut. I wasn't a loudmouth. I'd done it.

After all the MRIs, major diagnostic tests, and surgery, suddenly one day that prayer popped in my head out of the blue. I had completely forgotten.

God reminded me I was done. From the moment I remembered that thought, I was done. I didn't make the announcement for eight more weeks, but I knew I was done. In August 1999 it was time to move on. I was almost 33 years old. I had no second thoughts. My deal with God was complete and He was a Gentleman for keeping His end of the deal.

I interviewed with Merrill Lynch and Morgan Stanley in September 1999, and received offers from both. Since I had a better feel about Morgan Stanley, I chose to go work for that firm.

I didn't want to be around big egos in sports anymore. I'd been exposed to both extremes; I'd enjoyed a lot of public acknowledgment and media coverage, and I'd been totally ignored. Somewhere between the two is nice. I don't want either extreme anymore.

•   •   •

I'd confided in Tom Zupancic in Indy about my disease. He was a good friend and somebody I could trust. Then one day he needed my help. He told me about a "high profile friend" who was in trouble with narcotics. He couldn't stop. Tom asked me what he should do.

"He needs to get treatment and start going to AA." For me the answer was simple and clear. Tom thanked me and we dropped the subject.

Several months later, I walked into an AA meeting and was startled to see Tom's friend. We recognized each other. I realized then he was the one Tom had been talking about. We sat together during the meeting and made small talk. I didn't want to call attention to his being a newcomer there. We exchanged telephone numbers and enjoyed the meeting.

Several months later, he called me on my cell phone. He needed help.

"I'm in trouble," he cried. "I just can't stop and I'm gonna kill myself with this stuff!"

I was in my office at Morgan Stanley when I got that call. I interrupted my work and called my sponsor. One of the AA rules is never to go on a 12-step call alone. This was a 12-step call, and I couldn't risk getting drunk or high again, so my sponsor went with me.

When we got to his house, we talked for several hours. He agreed to go to a meeting with us, so the three of us found the nearest one and headed off. That route was a successful—albeit temporary—one for him. By the time I left Indy, he'd been eight months sober. I sponsored him and I feel that was one of the finer things I've done in life.

My life was finally about being able to help someone else. He was dealing with his own demons. I held his hand for a few months, and then I needed to move on.

I learned four months after I left Indy that he was back to drinking and drugging. He'd stopped doing the right things. After two more years, he went into treatment two more times, and now has been sober for the past five years. That's pretty typical for most of us drunks. *The disease doesn't discriminate and it never gives up. All we can do is live "one day at a time."*

• • •

The stock market was hot and investments were doling out great returns. I'd been calling all the shots about where I wanted my money, so I worked with Morgan Stanley for 15 months. I soon discovered it's different when you're dealing with others' money. I hated to be in the position where my clients were losing money, no matter what I did. Silicon Valley and the NASDAQ began their rapid decline that year, and the opportunity to manage a golf course near home in Ontario surfaced. I gave two weeks' notice, and moved to Canada in October 2000.

Then, within a few short years, God brought another miracle in to my life, one I had already given up on.

Char and I hadn't given each other any thought during more than a decade of living our separate lives. We dated almost two years in college, then drifted apart, each of us pursuing relationships with other people. But coincidently in recent years, we both experienced life-changing events. Each of us discovered a center of spirituality that now guides our daily living. We both now believe the hand of God was working in our lives; we just didn't know it at the time. He even had to rap on our shoulders, more than once, to get our attention. We're both a little hardheaded, so sometimes it takes several raps to get our attention.

In February 1999, I took a few days off and traveled to Las Vegas with my then-current girlfriend. We planned to hit the tables and see some shows and hang out in Vegas for three or four days. Little did I know, Char and some girlfriends also planned a trip to Las Vegas, at the same time, to take in a hunter-jumper association World Cup horse show. She is an accomplished rider, and the World Cup touts the best on the globe. My girlfriend and I were walking through the MGM Grand, mid-afternoon, when I suddenly bumped into someone. It was Char.

She and two friends were walking through the MGM Grand; Char was in the middle, moving her head back and forth, chatting away and paying no attention to where she was going. She bumped directly into my 6'6" frame.

She looked up. I looked down.

"...Tony?" The look on her face was incredulous. Mine probably was too.

My girlfriend grabbed my arm and yanked me away.

I stopped after several steps and looked back at Char. She stopped and looked back at me. The girlfriend yanked my arm again and we left the MGM Grand.

That's all that happened, but we both remembered it. We were both flabbergasted. After all those years, we still lived and existed in the same universe.

Char returned to Arizona and continued to live her life. Three years later, she told a friend what happened at the MGM Grand. Char wondered aloud with her friend about what was going on in my life. Her friend suggested she 'put it out in the universe, and the response will come back to you'. So she did. Two months later, she listened to MSU's NCAA tournament basketball game on her headphones at her son's baseball practice. Another parent asked what she was listening to; she told him and his response got her attention: "My best friend has a best friend who went to MSU in the late 1980s. Wonder if you know him?"

Char's response, "Yah, sure" ... like she knew all 40,000 students there in the late 1980s.

"He's Tony Mandarich!" Char didn't know how to respond, and kept quiet.

Two weeks later, the guy's wife approached Char. She'd recognized Char's non-response.

"You DID know Tony, didn't you?" It was more rhetorical than questioning. She continued, "I have some information about him. He's doing really well; he lives in Canada on a golf course and is married to a nice girl. We saw him a couple of months ago and he's really doing great."

Char responded this time. "That's really good to know; I'm happy for him." She had no thoughts of any future contact. The part about me being married was wrong, but Char didn't know that.

Another girlfriend of hers heard that conversation and took matters into her own hands. She called me, didn't identify herself, and said we had a mutual friend. I was busy but asked where the friend lived.

"In Arizona," she replied. She still hadn't identified herself.

"Well, if we have a mutual friend in Arizona, it has to be a girl, and can only be one person, Charlavan." She'd gotten my attention.

She confirmed my guess and told me Char didn't know she was contacting me. I gave her my email address saying she could give it to Char to contact me via the Internet if she wanted.

On Char's birthday a few days later, she gave Char a piece of paper on which was written my email address.

"What's this?" queried Char.

"Tony Mandarich's email address. I got his name, Googled® it on the Internet, called him, and he ended up giving me his email address to give you."

Char reports that it seemed odd to her at the time. As we look back on the series of incidents, it's clear to us that God's hand was guiding each incident. The information about how to contact me literally landed in Char's lap after she put it out to the universe. It was that rap on the shoulder thing.

We reconnected on Internet, and after several months of communicating, we both realized we needed to address our domestic relationships and issues before we pursued a relationship between us. We stopped communicating for another year, and on my birthday, I received a Happy Birthday greeting from Char. My domestic relationship had ended and Char's marriage was in its last stages. We reunited early in 2004 and were married May 5, 2004 in Niagara Falls.

Our life together began in the small cottage I'd been living in on Century Pines Golf Course in Troy, Ontario. Char and I each share custody of our children with our first spouses. Holly and Brittney (born after sobriety) live with their mother during the school year, and Char's kids, Alec and Ani, lived with their father during the school year. That first summer found all six of us making peace with each other daily in that little home. Although some moments were tense, we seemed to find a way to laugh about the difficult times and get through them with humor and respect. Austin Murphy came that June, along with two photographers, to do the "Where Are They Now?" story featured in Sports Illustrated, July 19, 2004. After 12 years, I decided to give SI another chance. I'll always be grateful to Austin for writing a fair, unbiased and not-nasty story about my football career. Thanks, Austin.

Char and I returned to Michigan State University for a visit in 2005. The old weight room had been moved to a new location. In that room players were tested on foot speed, bench press and squat weight. When I first walked in to that weight room in 1984, I promised myself my name would be posted on the board that touted the strongest players and best statistics before I left MSU. It was. And when my name was up on that board, there were other guys' names from 15 years back. In 2005, when Char and I visited the new weight room, I observed that the current team members' names were the only ones on the board, and none of them had the stats I had. I benched 545, and just missed 585 in that old room. My squat numbers were good too, and I could run really fast. Apparently the philosophy of posting names has changed, because there weren't any old names up on that board. Oh well, it gave me some pleasure to remind myself they hadn't been back to the Rose Bowl since I was there either!

The Colts rank #1 in my list of NFL favorite teams. They gave me a second chance, believing in me even before I was able to do so myself. As I watched the playoff game in January 2007 between the Colts and the Patriots, my heart swelled with pride for my historical connection with the Indianapolis Colts organization. We all whooped with elation when the game ended with the Colts winning 38-31. The only mission left, as my friend and Colts Owner Jim Irsay said on national TV as he accepted the Lamar Hunt Trophy (AFC Championship), was Super Bowl® LXI in Miami in two weeks. When my favorite team went on to win Super Bowl® LXI on Sunday, February 4, 2007, Char and I were there to enjoy the victory and celebrate with our friends in the Colts' organization.

I still believe if you want to be better than the best, you cannot do common things. I still want to be extraordinary. I love the photography and Internet business, and the way it makes me feel. I love to see what comes out of the camera and on the computer screen. Our clients absolutely love what we do; I get the greatest thrill from their excitement and joy with pictures we create for them and web sites that become the foundation for their businesses.

In our business, I search for ways to move farther along in artistic skill and business acumen. I need to be better than I was yesterday. I watch video tips, do online training programs and update our portfolio constantly. I'm doing shots of flowers today because I realize it's not as easy as throwing a flower in front of a camera and shooting. I learned how *not* to do that. I use a lot of discipline in my work, just as I did when I trained to play football. Right now, being happy and content with my life is what counts. I'm happy and satisfied with what I do. And I'm staying sober.

Without sobriety, nothing else matters. Photography, kids, Char... nothing matters if I'm drunk. I get up every morning thinking about staying connected with what's important in my *AA Big Book*, self-help and metaphysical books... always striving to stay connected. I keep trying to learn more about myself, about who

Tony Mandarich really is. I sat around for too many years expecting something good to happen. It didn't work. *I* wasn't changing, so nothing good was happening. I despised that part of me.

I still want the edge. Before sobriety, the edge was chemicals. Now, the edge is my spirit and my ability to love life and who I am.

Life's Lessons

The lessons I've learned in life are priceless. Sure, I'd like to say I played for 15 years, had a great career, won awards and accolades… but that's not my story. I'm content with who I am today. It is because of the adversities I've experienced that I am where I am. I *like* who I am today and I'm comfortable in my own skin. Adversity is a part of life and I don't regret what happened. It's not the perfect, fairytale story. My life was full of ups and downs, extreme highs and extreme lows. I was really at the top of the world with football. I experienced personal tragedy, death, marriage and divorce. If I had the choice, I'd have chosen nice and smooth. But at 42, I don't regret my life. My history has made me who I am today. I was in the public eye so my story gets attention. I know now that houses, cars, trips, celebrity, and money are the unimportant things in life; my sobriety and family are what's important now. And I'm willing to bet a dozen or so of my neighbors have had similar experiences. Because I've been in the public eye, I can tell my story and try to make an impact and help people.

This book is for those of you who are still out there drinking and drugging, dying a miserable, slow death. I have some suggestions for you. I hope you listen; you have nothing to lose. You've read my story; now I want to tell you what I have learned from my addictions. I hope it resonates.

Look In The Mirror. What do you see? Some of us are still ignoring the possibility we are addicted. I did that for seven years. That inner peace we seek in the bottle, pill or syringe is fake. It has no substance. It is a mirage in the desert. It lacks truth, honesty and most of all FREEDOM. You know something is missing, and cannot define that something. You will tell yourself this book isn't for you, nor is it about you. I ask you to look at the similarities and not the differences in our paths of addiction. My story is extended to you, here and now. Keep reading, and compare your story to mine until you finish. This could be your story, your life, as much as it is mine. The only difference between us is that I had to grow up in the public eye and make my mistakes there. You and I are no different; we put our pants on one leg at a time. My hand is extended to you even if you turn away now; perhaps this will plant a seed of hope, and one day you will come back to grasp that hope and dig your fingernails in it.

Admit powerlessness over drugs and alcohol. The only way I could beat them was to accept that I was powerless over them. In spite of what the media said, I fell on my face because of drugs and alcohol, not because of steroids. Doing the steroids was against all the rules, but I wasn't addicted to them. I had to separate what I read about me in the media with what I knew was happening. My dirty little secret was drugs and alcohol, and they were stronger and more powerful than I could ever be.

Addictions are life threatening; you are playing with Death when you continue using. My addictions almost killed me, and the same thing will surely happen with you if you continue to use. My full-time job was doing it, getting it, conning, chasing, and hiding it from employers and family. Being an alcoholic and drug addict is a full time job. Football was my part time job, and I failed miserably at Green Bay. We all will fail miserably with everything that's important to us if we continue on that path. You will be responsible for untold misery in the lives of other people, just as I was. I can finally say that I am responsible for the grief people felt over my performance and my behavior, and I am sorry for that grief.

Don't allow others' excuses (or your own) to cloud your vision. You cannot live a productive life if you drink and drug uncontrollably. Lindy Infante referred to me as the phenom of all phenoms; that's ego food. I allowed that kind of thinking to cloud my vision, to make me think there was no one like me in the world. I was invincible, and people like that can do anything they want and get away with it. I was an untouchable.

That thinking created very dense clouds in my path of vision. I joined in the hype. I believed I could do anything I wanted, including drugs and alcohol, and not be touched. I was totally out of touch with reality.

I was physically very large, so I created larger-than-life hype, and it became a media circus. I tried to play off that persona to create more fuss and spin and publicity. I wanted people to talk and push the draft idea so I would get more money and be drafted higher.

In retrospect, some of it, most of it, worked. However, I had to perform too. Hype alone doesn't block Reggie White. The media wrote everything I said and I had them in the palm of my hand. I remember plotting in my head about the next outrageous thing I could do or say without going too far. Once I was on the cover of SI, it was national hype and everybody in the country knew who I was. The combination of the hype and my near record-breaking performance at MSU and the NFL Combine positioned me to make NFL history. My alcoholism and drug addiction had other plans for me.

Bottom line: I don't believe *anybody* could ever have lived up to all of the hype I created and others fueled. I didn't then, and I couldn't have even without chemicals. And it was the chemicals that kept the fire going and my vision blurred.

Ask for, and accept, help. Before sobriety, it was always me against the world. I really believed everyone was against me and I believed I had to *fight* with everyone for my place in this world and in history. Life is so different now. I realize there are people genuinely out there to help me and want nothing *but* to help me. *Amazing!*

However, I had to get to the point that I knew I couldn't do it on my own. You have to admit that to yourself. Once we've done that, family and close friends, and comrades in AA and NA usually fall all over themselves trying to help. Some people can stop abusing by going to groups. Others need professional treatment in a substance abuse treatment facility to detox and get on the path to sobriety. Everyone has to find the path that works for him or her, and we all have to remember that we can't do it alone.

Alcoholism and drug addiction is a progressive disease. It gets worse, never better. Even though I haven't had any drugs or alcohol since March 23, 1995, I know the disease has progressed in my body. My AA friends who relapsed and came back to talk about it told me how much worse that episode was than previous ones. I heard them. That's one of the reasons I still go to AA meetings; I need to be reminded what would happen to me if I risked my sobriety and took a drink or started popping pills. And I pray daily and thank God for the grace He has given me.

You aren't any different from me. If you have it, this disease will be with you all your life. Most of us need ongoing support to stay sober, and I believe the disease is easier to handle when we establish a continuing relationship with a 12-step program.

Define your passion. I still carry some arrogance, I suppose. I just don't want to be like everybody else. I don't want to be average; I want to be in the top percentile. I want to set the curve, not land in the morass of the middle. Just as I wanted then to set the standard for football, now I want to set the standard for photography and Internet marketing, my current passions. I want to learn more every day. I don't want to produce an average product or service. I want to be the best, so I work to ensure what I produce isn't average.

I talk with friends all the time about my passion. I think about it constantly. I ask myself what is really important to me? What value, experience, activity, belief defines who I am more than anything else in the world? If you can figure out what that is, and then carry it around with you in your heart, you realize it's a big part of what creates your essence and makes you unique.

Live just one day at a time. I try not to use "never" and "always". Such declarations set parameters that suggest I might have the addictions licked, and whenever I've slipped and said 'never' or 'always', it comes back to haunt me. When I was so angry with my dad about the divorce, I said I'd *never* talk to him again; he's an asshole so I don't have to relate to him. Then four years later, after sobriety, I found myself driving 400 miles to see him and make amends. *I* was wrong, not my father. So I've tried to stop using those meaningless words.

Everyone has words like that in their lives. Living in the present moment just makes life more meaningful. Life became so much easier to live when I decided to just take one day at a time, when I realized I didn't have to manage the next few days or weeks or months before they arrived. It's amazing to me how much easier life is when lived one day at a time.

My deal is, I don't want to drink today. I ask God to keep me sober today. I thank God at night for keeping me sober.

Sobriety is Freedom. The most important part of recovery, besides physical sobriety, is the maintenance program you implement one day at a time. In those 17 days in the hospital, I realized I would go to meetings, contrary to what I told Amber on the drive to Brighton, and I would do it for the rest of my life. It's a choice. I listened to the professionals. My life depends on it. I listened to other recovering addicts who were sober and happy, some for years and some just months. My life depends on it.

A little humility never hurts anyone. In my case I needed a lot. I am still learning the virtue of humility. My life depends on me being humble about what I do and who I am. I strive daily to maintain a spiritual connection with the universe. I try to treat people with kindness, love and respect, the way I want to be treated. When I was in Green Bay, I treated people harshly and brashly, and that's what I got in return. After sobriety, when the fog in my head cleared, I could see what I'd done, and I changed. I saw that if I treated people honorably, I'd be treated the same way. I work every day to attract that into my life. You REAP what you SOW!

Making Amends. I returned to have fun playing football. I had nothing to lose and everything to gain. I think we all have to know how we are wired, what is important to us as individuals. When I began my comeback, the press referred to my past 'failures'; what they didn't know was how close to death I stumbled just a year previously. Being afraid of failure was the last thing on my mind. Making amends meant I needed to *try* to play again, and play *sober*. I had to do my best, give it everything I had. *That* was making amends.

After we become sober, we have to decide to whom we need to make amends. It's one of the 12 steps necessary for recovery. Then we have to get serious about telling them how we wronged them. Most of the time, it is family and friends. Sometimes it's a group of people. For me it was all of the above and football fans across the country. Everyone has to figure that out for him or herself, and make amends to recognize their wrongdoing and not do it again.

As I write this at age 42, I don't do any second-guessing; I'm not forever wondering if I *could* have played sober. I *did* play sober, and I played well. Gary Myers, sportswriter for The New York Daily News, wrote,

> "Mandarich knows he's writing a pretty neat story. 'To me, that's a detail,' he said. 'For me, it's already been a successful comeback. I've met great people, been around great players, there's been great camaraderie and I've had a blast doing it so far. I said before the final cut that, if cut, to me it has already been successful.'"[28]

I made amends; I slew my demons. And now I've written the story that finally tells the truth. I still make mistakes, and I keep trying to learn from them. I hope you slay your demons and write your own stories; learn from your mistakes. I didn't get or maintain my sobriety because I played football. I became sober with the Grace of God, the help of members of AA, and because I had the willingness to take action and do the things that had to be done.

If this story has helped one of you to recognize that you need help, it was worth all the media controversy. Keep trudging the High Road of Happy Destiny!

---

[28] Myers, Gary. *New York Daily News*. "The Twice is Right: Mandarich Basks in Second Chance." September 6, 1996.

I had this poem posted in my locker the three years I played at Indy. It's one of my favorites.

The Grasp of Your Hand

Let me not pray to be sheltered from dangers,
but to be fearless in facing them.

Let me not beg for the stilling of my pain,
but for the heart to conquer it.

Let me not crave in anxious fear to be saved,
but hope for the patience to win my freedom.

Grant me that I may not be a coward, feeling
Your mercy in my success alone; but let me find
the grasp of Your hand in my failure.

—Rabindranath Tagore (1861-1941)

About Tony Mandarich

Tony Mandarich was born in Oakville, Ontario, Canada, the son of Croatian immigrants who instilled in him a grit and determination to accomplish the impossible. Tony grew up with a love for football, and decided early in his life that he would play professionally. After a highly successful and nationally publicized collegiate career at Michigan State University, Tony was drafted number two overall in 1989 by the Green Bay Packers. The hype about being "the best offensive line prospect ever", along with Tony's addictions, was more than he could live up to, and his life came crashing down around him. After three more years of alcohol and painkiller abuse, Tony accepted the hand of God, went into treatment and now considers it a privilege to be able to help other addicts and alcoholics when called upon. Tony and his wife, Charlavan, have four children; they own and operate Mandarich Media Group, LLC, in Scottsdale, AZ, a full-service web media business specializing in web site development and optimization, video production, photography and Internet marketing.

About Sharon Shaw Elrod

Sharon Shaw Elrod was born and raised in Iowa, completing college degrees at the University of Northern Iowa (BA in Education), University of Nebraska (MSW) and Nova Southeastern University (EdD in Educational Leadership). Following a career in education and social work, she settled into retirement in the Piney Woods of East Texas with her husband, Jerry. Sharon returned to the post-retirement work force as a writer and author. Her first book, *Shar's Story: a Mother and*  *Daughter Reunited* (2005), was a finalist in the prestigious North Texas Book Festival, 2007. Sharon and her husband divide their time between East Texas and Scottsdale, Arizona.

References

AA Services. *Alcoholics Anonymous: Big Book, Fourth Edition.* New York: Alcoholics Anonymous World Services, Inc.

Bansch, J. (December 18, 1996). Colts Put Credit on Offensive Line. *Indianapolis Star.*

Barnas, J. (April 4, 1996) Tony Mandarich Eyeing NFL Comeback. *Detroit Free Press.*

Buchsbaum, J. (July 28, 1996). Scout's Notebook. *Pro Football Weekly.*

Chappell, M. (February 23, 1996). Colts Willing to Take Chance on Mandarich. *Indianapolis Star.*

Chappell, M. (August 2, 1996). Mandarich Makes Headway in his Comeback. *Indianapolis Star.*

Chappell, M. (November 23, 1996). Mathews Will Tackle Left Side to Make Room for Mandarich. *Indianapolis Star.*

Chappell, M. (August, 1997). Colts' Mandarich Not Getting Too Comfortable. *Indianapolis Star.*

Chopra, D. *Fire in the Heart.* New York: Simon Pulse.

Havel, C.. (November 14, 1992). Second Opinion Backs Up the First. *Green Bay Press Gazette.*

Howard, J. (October 30, 1992). Ill Feelings Mystify Mandarich. *Detroit Free Press*

Lowenkron, H. (June 12, 1998). Mandarich Big Part of Rejuvenated Line. *Johnson County Daily Journal.*

McGinn, B. (October 27, 1992). Answer Sought at Mayo. *Milwaukee Journal Sentinel.*

Mandarich's Brother Dies of Cancer. *Milwaukee Journal Sentinel.*

Mulhern, T. (January, 1993). Packer Commentary: Mandarich Saga Will Soon Be Over. *Milwaukee Journal Sentinel.*

Myers, G. (September 6, 1996). The Twice is Right: Mandarich Basks in Second Chance. *New York Daily News.*

O'Hara, M. (April 26, 1996). Mandarich Tries Comeback, Looking for a Better Ending. *The Detroit News.*

O'Hara, M. (November 20, 1997). Mandarich Learned His Lesson. *The Detroit News.*

Pierson, D. (December 26, 1996). An Attitude Adjustment in Indy. *Chicago Tribune.*

Zimmerman, P. (April 24, 1989). Mandarich as the Pros See Him. *Sports Illustrated.*

Recommended Reading

A.A. Services (2001) *Alcoholics Anonymous: Big Book. (4th Ed.)* Alcoholics Anonymous World Services, Inc.

Allen, J. (2002) *As a Man Thinketh*. Deseret Book Company.

Ames, R.T. /translator (1993) *Sun-Tzu: The art of war: the first English translation incorporating the recently discovered Yin-ch' üeh-shan texts*. New York, NY: Ballantine Books.

"C", Chuck (1984) *A New Pair of Glasses*. Irvine, CA: New Look Publishing.

Chopra, D. (1994) *The Seven Spiritual Laws of Success*. San Rafael, CA: Amber-Allen Publishing. Novato, CA: New World Library.

Chopra, D. (2006) *Power, freedom, and grace: living from the source of lasting happiness*. San Rafael, CA: Amber-Allen Publishing.

Cleary, T.F./translator (1993) *Zen Lessons: The Art of Leadership*. Boston, MA: Shambhala Publications, Inc.

Dalai Lama (1998) *The Art of Happiness: A Handbook for Living*. Penguin Group (USA)

Hawking, S. (1988) *A Brief History of Time*. New York, NY: Bantam Books.

Nhat Hanh, T. (1991) *Peace Is Every Step: The path of Mindfulness in Everyday Life*. New York, NY: Bantam Books.

Redfield, J. (1994) *The Celestine Prophecy*. Grand Central Publishing.

Stevens, J.L. (2005) *Praying with power: How to use ancient shamanic techniques to gain maximum spiritual benefit and extraordinary results through prayer*. London, UK: Watkins Publishing.

Thoreau, H.D. (2004) *Walden*. Beacon Press.

Tolle, E. (1999) *The Power of Now: A Guide to Spiritual Enlightenment*. Novato, Ca: New World Library.

Trungpa,C. (1991) *Meditation in Action.* Boston, MA: Shambhala
    Publications, Inc.

Trungpa, C. (2003) *Shambhala: Sacred Path of the Warrior.* Boston, MA:
    Shambhala Publications, Inc.

Vetter, H. /editor (1997) *The Heart of God: Prayers of Rabindranath
    Tagore.* Boston, MA: Tuttle Publishing.

Whitman, W. (2002) *Leaves of Grass and Other Writings.* Norton, W. W.
    & Company, Inc.

Wolf, F.A. (2004) *Dr. Quantum Presents: Meet the Real Creator – You!*
    Sounds True, Incorporated. (compact disc set)

Index

Printed in the United States
219414BV00002B/9/P

9 781932 690781